THE PUB QUIZ BOOK 3
Burns & Porter Associates

CORGI BOOKS

PRINTING HISTORY

A CORGI BOOK 0 552 133396

First publication in Great Britain

This book is set in 10/11 pt Univers

Corgi Books are published by Transworld Publishers Ltd., 61–63 Uxbridge Road, Ealing, London W5 5SA, in Australia by Transworld Publishers (Australia) Pty. Ltd., 15–23 Helles Avenue, Moorebank, NSW 2170, and in New Zealand by Transworld Publishers (N.Z.) Ltd., Cnr. Moselle and Waipareira Avenues, Henderson, Auckland.

Printed and bound in Great Britain by
Cox & Wyman Ltd, Reading

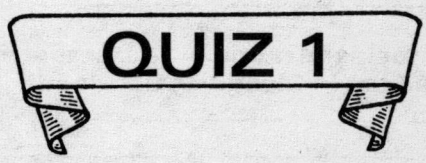

QUIZ 1

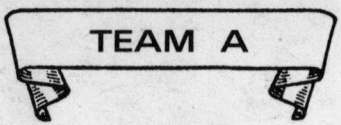

TEAM A

ROUND ONE
(Team Questions)

1 Q: What is the name of the largest soccer stadium in Glasgow, Scotland?

A: _ _ _ _ _ _ _ _ _ _ _ _ _ _ _ _ (p. 122)

●

2 Q: In terms of angle measurement how many degrees are there in a turn and a half?

A: _ _ _ _ _ _ _ _ _ _ _ _ _ _ _ _ (p. 122)

3 Q: Which continental golfer won the Epson (not Epsom) Matchplay Championship in 1987?

A: _ _ _ _ _ _ _ _ _ _ _ _ _ _ _ _ (p. 122)

●

4 Q: What substance found in every home has the chemical formula $C12\ H22\ O11$?

A: _ _ _ _ _ _ _ _ _ _ _ _ _ _ _ _ (p. 122)

HOW TO PLAY

This book contains five complete general knowledge quiz matches. It is possible to use it in two ways:

Solo Play

If you want to test your general knowledge on your own, simply write down the answers to the various questions in the space provided underneath. At the end of each round turn to the relevant page in the Answer section at the back of the book to check to see if you were right.

Team Play

For this you need at least two players. If there are only two of you one of you must hold the book and ask the questions, looking up the answers in the relevant section of the book after each question. If you like you may time your opponent giving him or her a maximum of 30 seconds per question. Once your round is over, pass the book to your opponent and they will ask *you* the questions! If you have an odd number of players, one person may be nominated umpire, timekeeper and scorer while the others are split into even numbered teams. In this case only the umpire need hold the book. If a team fails to answer a question in thirty seconds or gets the answer wrong, then the umpire will throw the question open to the opposing team who will have 15 seconds to answer.

2 points are awarded for a correct answer from the first team.
1 point is awarded to the second team if they get an answer that the first team couldn't answer.

Some questions are specified *team* questions and others *individual* questions. Take it in turns to answer *individual* questions if you have more than one person per team.

Each quiz has eight rounds of eight questions per team. There are also sixteen 'friendly' questions at the end of each quiz. These are meant to relax the players after the excitement of the competition questions. However, if you have a tied match you can use them as tie-breakers. The answers to the friendly questions will be found at the back of the book.

Burns and Porter's approved method of match play is for two teams of four players, two people as scorers/ timekeepers and one person as question-master.
   Each match should last about an hour.

The Burns & Porter Pub Quiz Book 3 contains five fact-filled quizzes which will improve not only your own general knowledge but your family's as well:

DO YOU KNOW:
The name given to the art of decorating or engraving the bones of whales?
The group name for wild geese in flight?
The name of the male star of the 1978 movie 'Grease'?

Burns and Porter Associates are Europe's leading Pub Quiz organisers. In addition to providing 5000 UK teams with quizzes, they regularly supply them to radio and TV programmes.

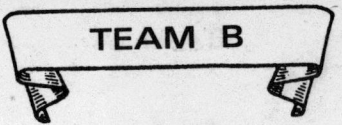

TEAM B

ROUND ONE
(Team Questions)

---

1 Q: The Traitor's Gate is part of which
   famous building in Britain?

   A: _ _ _ _ _ _ _ _ _ _ _ _ _ _ _ _ (p. 124)

---●---

2 Q: The S.I. unit of a joule is a measurement
   of what, specifically?

   A: _ _ _ _ _ _ _ _ _ _ _ _ _ _ _ _ (p. 124)

---●---

3 Q: In 1985 the United States lost the
   Ryder Cup golf tournament for the first
   time since. . . . when?

   A: _ _ _ _ _ _ _ _ _ _ _ _ _ _ _ _ (p. 124)

---●---

4 Q: Which chemical element is represented
   by the letter 'F'?

   A: _ _ _ _ _ _ _ _ _ _ _ _ _ _ _ _ (p. 124)

---●---

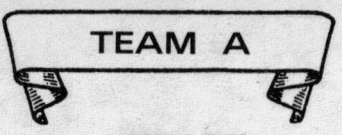

ROUND TWO
(Team Questions)

1 Q: Which former British Prime Minister was appointed a Knight of the Garter in April 1976?

A: _ _ _ _ _ _ _ _ _ _ _ _ _ _ _ _ _ (p. 126)

2 Q: The owner of The Times newspaper died in August 1976. What was his name?

A: _ _ _ _ _ _ _ _ _ _ _ _ _ _ _ _ _ (p. 126)

3 Q: On which island, in March 1977, did two Jumbo Jets collide in what was claimed to be the world's worst aircraft disaster?

A: _ _ _ _ _ _ _ _ _ _ _ _ _ _ _ _ _ (p. 126)

4 Q: Which British driver won the Grand Prix World Drivers' Championship in 1976?

A: _ _ _ _ _ _ _ _ _ _ _ _ _ _ _ _ (p. 126)

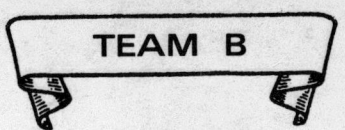

TEAM B

ROUND TWO
(Team Questions)

1 Q: Who became Britain's Prime Minister in April 1976?

A: _ _ _ _ _ _ _ _ _ _ _ _ _ _ (p. 128)

———————— ● ————————

2 Q: In November 1976, the American oilgroup Atlantic Richfield took control of which National British newspaper?

A: _ _ _ _ _ _ _ _ _ _ _ _ _ _ (p. 128)

———————— ● ————————

3 Q: Which country was affected, in July 1976, by the world's worst earthquake (in terms of number killed) for over four hundred years?

A: _ _ _ _ _ _ _ _ _ _ _ _ _ _ _ (p. 128)

———————— ● ————————

4 Q: Who, in 1976, became the first British male since 1908 to win an Olympic swimming Gold Medal?

A: _ _ _ _ _ _ _ _ _ _ _ _ _ _ (p. 128)

———————— ● ————————

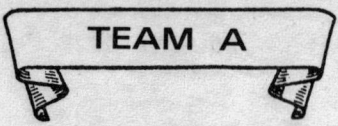

TEAM A

---

1 Q: What computer programming language is named after a 17th century French mathematician who, at the age of 19 invented the first adding machine?

   A: _ _ _ _ _ _ _ _ _ _ _ _ _ _ _ (p. 130)

   ───────────── ● ─────────────

2 Q: Which English peninsula is formed by the estuaries of the Mersey and the Dee?

   A: _ _ _ _ _ _ _ _ _ _ _ _ _ _ _ (p. 130)

   ───────────── ● ─────────────

3 Q: What are Ishihara charts used to determine?

   A: _ _ _ _ _ _ _ _ _ _ _ _ _ _ _ (p. 130)

   ───────────── ● ─────────────

4 Q: On a coat of arms what did a 'bend sinister' signify?

   A: _ _ _ _ _ _ _ _ _ _ _ _ _ _ _ (p. 130)

   ───────────── ● ─────────────

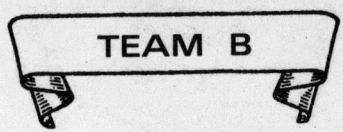

TEAM B

ROUND THREE
(Individual Questions: No conferring by either side)

1 Q: Who worked for nearly forty years on
the uncompleted 'Difference Engine', a
19th century fore-runner of the analytic
computer?

A: _ _ _ _ _ _ _ _ _ _ _ _ _ _ _ _ _ (p. 132)

●

2 Q: What is the area of water flanked by
Gibraltar Point and Hunstanton Point
known as?

A: _ _ _ _ _ _ _ _ _ _ _ _ _ _ _ _ _ (p. 132)

●

3 Q: Who was the English physicist, a
sufferer himself, who first described
colour blindness?

A: _ _ _ _ _ _ _ _ _ _ _ _ _ _ _ _ _ (p. 132)

●

4 Q: In heraldry, what does the term 'dexter'
mean?

A: _ _ _ _ _ _ _ _ _ _ _ _ _ _ _ _ _ (p. 132)

●

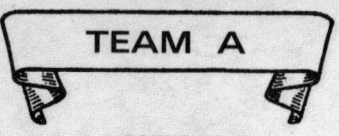

TEAM A

ROUND FOUR
(Team Questions)

1 Q: Which British Prime Minister was
   famous for changing into evening dress
   before writing his novels?
   A: _ _ _ _ _ _ _ _ _ _ _ _ _ _ _ _ (p. 135)

2 Q: What is the most common family
   surname in the world, of which there
   are over 104 million people with the
   name?
   A: _ _ _ _ _ _ _ _ _ _ _ _ _ _ _ _ (p. 135)

3 Q: Which single word in the English
   language has the most meanings,
   having 58 noun, 126 verbal and 10
   partial adjective uses?
   A: _ _ _ _ _ _ _ _ _ _ _ _ _ _ _ _ (p. 135)

4 Q: Which fruit bears the largest known
   seed in the world, which may weigh up
   to 40 lb?
   A: _ _ _ _ _ _ _ _ _ _ _ _ _ _ _ _ (p. 135)

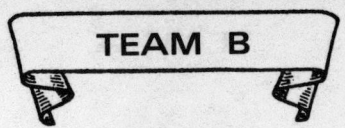

TEAM B

ROUND FOUR
(Team Questions)

1 Q: Which famous 19th century classical
    author could only write when facing
    north?

  A: _ _ _ _ _ _ _ _ _ _ _ _ _ _ _ _ _ (p. 138)

———————————●———————————

2 Q: What is the Indian family surname
    which means 'In Secret', of which
    there were 90,000 people with the
    name in Britain in 1984?

  A: _ _ _ _ _ _ _ _ _ _ _ _ _ _ _ _ (p. 138)

———————————●———————————

3 Q: Which single word in the English
    language has the most homophones
    (various spellings and meanings but
    pronounced the same)?

  A: _ _ _ _ _ _ _ _ _ _ _ _ _ _ _ _ (p. 138)

———————————●———————————

4 Q: Which tree bears the largest known
    leaves of any plant in the world, which
    may measure up to 65 ft. in length of
    the blade?

  A: _ _ _ _ _ _ _ _ _ _ _ _ _ _ _ _ (p. 138)

———————————●———————————

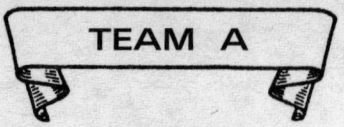

TEAM A

ROUND FIVE
(Team Questions)

---

1 Q: In horse-racing what is a male,
   ungelded horse up to four years old
   called?

   A: _ _ _ _ _ _ _ _ _ _ _ _ _ _ _ (p. 141)

   ────────────●────────────

2 Q: Who expanded her music business
   career into Hollywood in 1972 with her
   starring role in 'Lady Sings the Blues'?

   A: _ _ _ _ _ _ _ _ _ _ _ _ _ _ _ (p. 141)

   ────────────●────────────

3 Q: Which city is joined to Moscow by the
   trans-Siberian railway?

   A: _ _ _ _ _ _ _ _ _ _ _ _ _ _ _ (p. 141)

   ────────────●────────────

4 Q: In which country, in August 1987, was
   Prime Minister David Lange returned to
   power for a second three-year term?

   A: _ _ _ _ _ _ _ _ _ _ _ _ _ _ _ (p. 141)

   ────────────●────────────

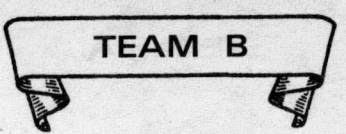

TEAM B

ROUND FIVE
(Team Questions)

1 Q: In horse-racing, what is a female horse up to four years old called?

A: _ _ _ _ _ _ _ _ _ _ _ _ _ _ _ _ _ (p. 144)

———————————— ● ————————————

2 Q: Which British rock star pursued his developing acting career in the 1978 film, 'Just a Gigolo'?

A: _ _ _ _ _ _ _ _ _ _ _ _ _ _ _ _ (p. 144)

———————————— ● ————————————

3 Q: Which city is the Southern Terminal for the 'Orient Express'?

A: _ _ _ _ _ _ _ _ _ _ _ _ _ _ _ _ (p. 144)

———————————— ● ————————————

4 Q: The Nazi Rudolf Hess died in August 1987, aged 93. In which prison was he held for 41 years?

A: _ _ _ _ _ _ _ _ _ _ _ _ _ _ _ _ (p. 144)

———————————— ● ————————————

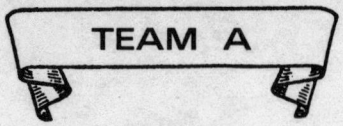

ROUND SIX
(Team Questions)

1 Q: What name is given to the rules which
govern the work of the House of
Commons in Britain?
A: _ _ _ _ _ _ _ _ _ _ _ _ _ _ _ _ (p. 147)

—————————————— ● ——————————————

2 Q: For what sporting event is the city of
Le Mans famous?
A: _ _ _ _ _ _ _ _ _ _ _ _ _ _ _ (p. 147)

—————————————— ● ——————————————

3 Q: Into which ocean does the Mackenzie
river flow?
A: _ _ _ _ _ _ _ _ _ _ _ _ _ _ _ (p. 147)

—————————————— ● ——————————————

4 Q: A 'descent' is the collective noun for
what type of bird?
A: _ _ _ _ _ _ _ _ _ _ _ _ _ _ _ (p. 147)

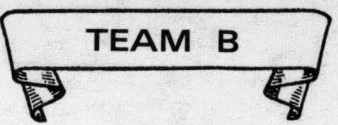

TEAM B

ROUND SIX
(Team Questions)

1 Q: What is the name given to the Pastoral staff or crook of a Bishop?

A: _ _ _ _ _ _ _ _ _ _ _ _ _ _ _ _ (p. 149)

●

2 Q: What is the popular name of the Australian National Rugby Union team?

A: _ _ _ _ _ _ _ _ _ _ _ _ _ _ _ _ (p. 149)

●

3 Q: Into which sea does the Volga river flow?

A: _ _ _ _ _ _ _ _ _ _ _ _ _ _ _ _ (p. 149)

●

4 Q: A 'plump' is the collective noun for what type of bird?

A: _ _ _ _ _ _ _ _ _ _ _ _ _ _ _ _ (p. 149)

●

INTERESTING FACT:
John Wesley once took refuge at the White Bear in Barrowford on an August day in 1748 when an angry mob turned on him when he was preaching at the village of Roughlee.

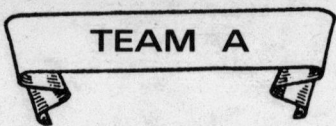

TEAM A

ROUND SEVEN
(Individual Questions: No conferring by either side)

1 Q: In what way is the Latin phrase
   'exempli gratia' more familiar to us?
   A: _ _ _ _ _ _ _ _ _ _ _ _ _ _ _ _ _ _ (p. 151)

⬤

2 Q: For what kind of painting did the
   English artist John Constable become
   most famous?
   A: _ _ _ _ _ _ _ _ _ _ _ _ _ _ _ _ _ _ (p. 151)

⬤

3 Q: Which actor was star of the 1984 U.S.
   film, 'The Natural', about a baseball
   hero?
   A: _ _ _ _ _ _ _ _ _ _ _ _ _ _ _ _ _ (p. 151)

⬤

4 Q: Who was Alexander the Great's
   famous tutor?
   A: _ _ _ _ _ _ _ _ _ _ _ _ _ _ _ _ _ (p. 151)

⬤

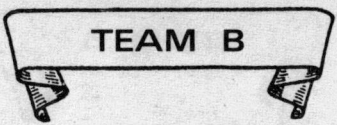

TEAM B

ROUND SEVEN
(Individual Questions: No conferring by either side)

1 Q: For what purpose is the French phrase
'Poste Restante' used in Britain?

A: _ _ _ _ _ _ _ _ _ _ _ _ _ _ _ _ (p. 153)

● ─────

2 Q: Which French artist made his name
with his posters advertising 'Les Follies
Bergeres' in Paris?

A: _ _ _ _ _ _ _ _ _ _ _ _ _ _ _ _ (p. 153)

● ─────

3 Q: Which actor was star of the 1984 U.S.
film, 'Tightrope', about a mass
murderer in New Orleans?

A: _ _ _ _ _ _ _ _ _ _ _ _ _ _ _ (p. 153)

● ─────

4 Q: Who was the author friend of James
Boswell about whom he wrote a
biography?

A: _ _ _ _ _ _ _ _ _ _ _ _ _ _ _ (p. 153)

●

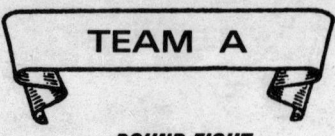

TEAM A

ROUND EIGHT
(Team Questions)

1 Q: Writer, Edgar Allan Poe, frequently
wrote with what balanced on his left
shoulder?

A: _ _ _ _ _ _ _ _ _ _ _ _ _ _ _ _ (p. 156)

2 Q: In which century was the game of
bowls, played on grass, started in
Britain?

A: _ _ _ _ _ _ _ _ _ _ _ _ _ _ _ _ (p. 156)

3 Q: The man-eating bellowing monster
inhabiting swamps and lagoons called
the 'Bunyip' is featured in the folk-lore
of which country?

A: _ _ _ _ _ _ _ _ _ _ _ _ _ _ _ _ (p. 156)

4 Q: Which English monarch was buried in a
square coffin?

A: _ _ _ _ _ _ _ _ _ _ _ _ _ _ _ _ (p. 156)

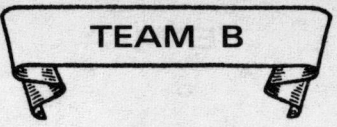

TEAM B

ROUND EIGHT
(Team Questions)

1 Q: What item of clothing or accessory did
the wife of Napoleon III, the Empress
Eugenie, never wear more than twice?

A: _ _ _ _ _ _ _ _ _ _ _ _ _ _ _ _ (p. 158)

●

2 Q: Which is traditionally the most popular
card game in Britain?

A: _ _ _ _ _ _ _ _ _ _ _ _ _ _ _ _ (p. 158)

●

3 Q: According to legend which is said to be
the only animal immune from the
deathly gaze of the cockatrice or
basilisk monster?

A: _ _ _ _ _ _ _ _ _ _ _ _ _ _ _ _ (p. 158)

●

4 Q: Which famous 19th century woman
carried a pet owl in her pocket
everywhere she went?

A: _ _ _ _ _ _ _ _ _ _ _ _ _ _ _ _ (p. 158)

●

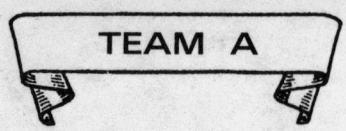

TEAM A

FRIENDLY QUESTIONS

---

1 Q: The leaf-shoots of which plant are
     called English Bamboo, after being
     boiled as a substitute for Asparagus?
  A: _ _ _ _ _ _ _ _ _ _ _ _ _ _ _ (p. 160)

---

2 Q: 'Sea-parrot' is an old sailor's name for
     what creature?
  A: _ _ _ _ _ _ _ _ _ _ _ _ _ _ _ (p. 160)

---

3 Q: British soldiers who had been training
     in which African country were the
     centre of an AIDS scare in January
     1987?
  A: _ _ _ _ _ _ _ _ _ _ _ _ _ _ _ (p. 160)

---

4 Q: What is the special property of a
     catalyst in chemical reactions?
  A: _ _ _ _ _ _ _ _ _ _ _ _ _ _ _ (p. 160)

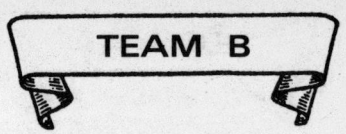

TEAM B

FRIENDLY QUESTIONS

---

1 Q: Which bird's nests are used to make
bird's-nest soup?

A: _ _ _ _ _ _ _ _ _ _ _ _ _ _ _ _ (p. 161)

———————— ● ————————

2 Q: What creature was referred to by
sailors as a 'sea-dog'?

A: _ _ _ _ _ _ _ _ _ _ _ _ _ _ _ _ (p. 161)

———————— ● ————————

3 Q: Which London Borough was revealed in
January 1987 as having the highest
rate of illegitimate births in the country?

A: _ _ _ _ _ _ _ _ _ _ _ _ _ _ _ (p. 161)

———————— ● ————————

4 Q: What dangerous gas is given off in a
blast furnace during manufacture of
pig-iron?

A: _ _ _ _ _ _ _ _ _ _ _ _ _ _ _ _ (p. 161)

———————— ● ————————

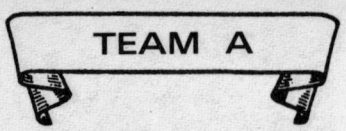

TEAM A

MORE FRIENDLY QUESTIONS

1 Q: What is a 'sinecure' (sin-e-cur)?
A: _ _ _ _ _ _ _ _ _ _ _ _ _ _ _ _ _ (p. 160)

2 Q: What is the other name for the musical
instrument the 'mouth-organ'?
A: _ _ _ _ _ _ _ _ _ _ _ _ _ _ _ _ _ (p. 160)

3 Q: What line follows 'Tho cowards flinch
and traitors sneer' from a well known
song?
A: _ _ _ _ _ _ _ _ _ _ _ _ _ _ _ _ _ (p. 160)

4 Q: In the Bible, on what day did God create
the Sun, Moon and stars?
A: _ _ _ _ _ _ _ _ _ _ _ _ _ _ _ _ _ (p. 160)

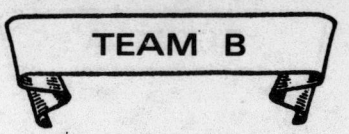

MORE FRIENDLY QUESTIONS

---

1 Q: What are 'Dundrearies'?
A: _ _ _ _ _ _ _ _ _ _ _ _ _ _ _ _ _ (p. 161)

---●---

2 Q: What does a first-nighter do?
A: _ _ _ _ _ _ _ _ _ _ _ _ _ _ _ _ _ (p. 161)

---●---

3 Q: Which politician said, 'When you stop a
dictator there are always risks. But
there are greater risks in not stopping a
dictator'?
A: _ _ _ _ _ _ _ _ _ _ _ _ _ _ _ _ (p. 161)

---●---

4 Q: Who, in the Bible, was asked to
interpret the 'Writing on the Wall'?
A: _ _ _ _ _ _ _ _ _ _ _ _ _ _ _ _ _ (p. 161)

---●---

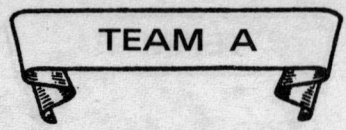

TEAM A

RESERVE QUESTIONS

---

1 Q: The actresses Sharon Gless and Tyne
Daley star as police in which American
T.V. series?

A: _ _ _ _ _ _ _ _ _ _ _ _ _ _ _ _ (p. 160)

───────────────● ───────────────

2 Q: Which nation administers the territory
of the Commonwealth of Puerto Rico?

A: _ _ _ _ _ _ _ _ _ _ _ _ _ _ _ (p. 160)

───────────────● ───────────────

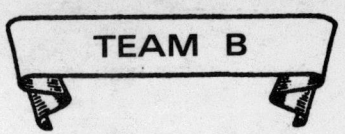

TEAM B

RESERVE QUESTIONS

1 Q: The actors Karl Malden and Michael
    Douglas starred together as police in
    which American T.V. series?
  A: _ _ _ _ _ _ _ _ _ _ _ _ _ _ _ _ _ (p. 161)

    ●

2 Q: What is the name of the Black Sea's
    only outlet?
  A: _ _ _ _ _ _ _ _ _ _ _ _ _ _ _ _ _ (p. 161)

    ●

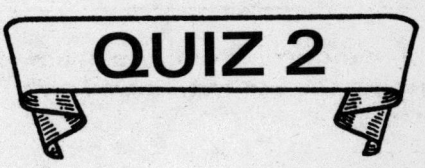

QUIZ 2

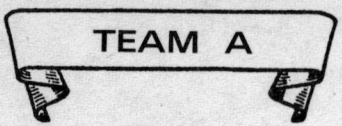

TEAM A

ROUND ONE
(Team Questions)

---

1 Q: Which mountain chain is deemed as forming the Eastern boundary to Europe?

A: _ _ _ _ _ _ _ _ _ _ _ _ _ _ _ (p. 122)

---•---

2 Q: What was the nationality of Sonja Henie, the figureskater, who died in 1969?

A: _ _ _ _ _ _ _ _ _ _ _ _ _ _ _ (p. 122)

---•---

3 Q: Who was the first English soccer player to have won over one hundred international caps?

A: _ _ _ _ _ _ _ _ _ _ _ _ _ _ _ (p. 122)

---•---

4 Q: What would you be suffering if you were treated with 'ignominy'?

A: _ _ _ _ _ _ _ _ _ _ _ _ _ _ _ (p. 122)

---•---

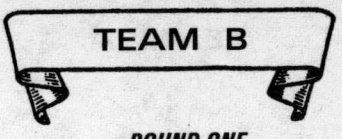

TEAM B

ROUND ONE
(Team Questions)

1 Q: In which ocean are the Maldive, Chagos and Cocos Islands situated?

A: _ _ _ _ _ _ _ _ _ _ _ _ _ _ _ (p. 124)

●

2 Q: What was the nationality of the World Heavyweight Boxing champion, Primo Carnera?

A: _ _ _ _ _ _ _ _ _ _ _ _ _ _ _ (p. 124)

●

3 Q: Who was the first soccer Footballer of the Year in 1946/7?

A: _ _ _ _ _ _ _ _ _ _ _ _ _ _ _ _ (p. 124)

●

4 Q: What does it mean to do something with 'celerity'?

A: _ _ _ _ _ _ _ _ _ _ _ _ _ _ _ _ (p. 124)

●

INTERESTING FACT:
The Old Wellington Inn in Manchester is thought to date back to the early 14th century.

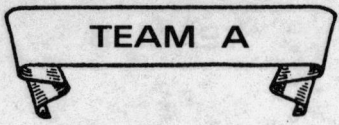

TEAM A

ROUND TWO
(Team Questions)

1 Q: 'It's Over' was a number one hit, in
Britain, in 1964, for which popular
singer?
A: _ _ _ _ _ _ _ _ _ _ _ _ _ _ _ _ (p. 126)

2 Q: Which tunnel between Switzerland and
Italy, was completed in March 1964?
A: _ _ _ _ _ _ _ _ _ _ _ _ _ _ _ _ (p. 126)

3 Q: When Harold Wilson formed a Labour
government in 1964, who was his first
Home Secretary?
A: _ _ _ _ _ _ _ _ _ _ _ _ _ _ _ _ (p. 126)

4 Q: Which British athlete won the women's
long jump at the 1964 Olympic Games?
A: _ _ _ _ _ _ _ _ _ _ _ _ _ _ _ _ (p. 126)

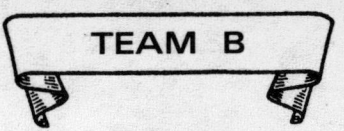

TEAM B

ROUND TWO
(Team Questions)

1 Q: The Kinks topped the British charts in 1964. Name the song they took to No. 1?

A: _ _ _ _ _ _ _ _ _ _ _ _ _ _ _ _ _ _ (p. 128)

──────────●──────────

2 Q: The Verrazano-Narrows Suspension Bridge was opened in November 1964. In which city is it?

A: _ _ _ _ _ _ _ _ _ _ _ _ _ _ _ _ _ (p. 128)

──────────●──────────

3 Q: Harold Wilson became British Prime Minister in 1964. Who was his first Foreign Secretary?

A: _ _ _ _ _ _ _ _ _ _ _ _ _ _ _ _ (p. 128)

──────────●──────────

4 Q: Which British athlete won the men's long jump at the 1964 Olympic Games?

A: _ _ _ _ _ _ _ _ _ _ _ _ _ _ _ _ (p. 128)

──────────●──────────

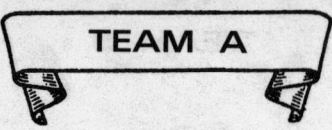

TEAM A

ROUND THREE
(Individual Questions: No conferring by either side)

1 Q: The U.S. composer Jerome Kern, wrote the music for which stage musical, first performed in 1927?

  A: _ _ _ _ _ _ _ _ _ _ _ _ _ _ _ _ (p. 130)

2 Q: Which famous person did Sirhan Sirhan assassinate?

  A: _ _ _ _ _ _ _ _ _ _ _ _ _ _ _ _ (p. 130)

3 Q: Who directed the films 'The Godfather' in 1972 and 'Apocalypse Now' in 1979?

  A: _ _ _ _ _ _ _ _ _ _ _ _ _ _ _ _ (p. 130)

4 Q: In what year did the British Labour party first form a government?

  A: _ _ _ _ _ _ _ _ _ _ _ _ _ _ _ _ (p. 130)

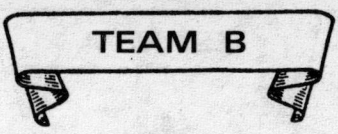

TEAM B

ROUND THREE
(Individual Questions: No conferring by either side)

1 Q: Lionel Bart wrote the words and music for which stage musical, first performed in London in 1960?

A: _ _ _ _ _ _ _ _ _ _ _ _ _ _ _ (p. 132)

2 Q: Which famous person was assassinated by James Earl Ray?

A: _ _ _ _ _ _ _ _ _ _ _ _ _ _ _ (p. 132)

3 Q: Who directed the films 'Jaws' in 1975 and 'Close Encounters of the Third Kind' in 1977?

A: _ _ _ _ _ _ _ _ _ _ _ _ _ _ _ (p. 132)

4 Q: In what year was the naval Battle of the River Plate?

A: _ _ _ _ _ _ _ _ _ _ _ _ _ _ (p. 132)

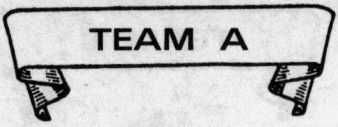

TEAM A

ROUND FOUR
(Team Questions)

1 Q: The rhyme entitled 'The Jackdaw of
      Rheims' is from which collection of
      poems and stories?
   A: _ _ _ _ _ _ _ _ _ _ _ _ _ _ _ _ (p. 135)

———————————●———————————

2 Q: Complete the following proverb 'Two's
      company. . . . . . .?
   A: _ _ _ _ _ _ _ _ _ _ _ _ _ _ _ _ (p. 135)

———————————●———————————

3 Q: In terms of transport what does the
      term cloverleaf apply to?
   A: _ _ _ _ _ _ _ _ _ _ _ _ _ _ _ _ (p. 135)

———————————●———————————

4 Q: Which British pop group's first number
      one single in the U.K. was called 'Down
      Down'?
   A: _ _ _ _ _ _ _ _ _ _ _ _ _ _ _ _ (p. 135)

———————————●———————————

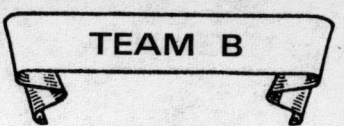

TEAM B

ROUND FOUR
(Team Questions)

1 Q: Who wrote the adventure novel 'The Last of the Mohicans'?

A: _ _ _ _ _ _ _ _ _ _ _ _ _ _ _ _ (p. 138)

2 Q: Complete the following saying 'Dead men tell. . . . .?

A: _ _ _ _ _ _ _ _ _ _ _ _ _ _ _ _ (p. 138)

3 Q: In terms of transport what is a 'permanent way' in Britain?

A: _ _ _ _ _ _ _ _ _ _ _ _ _ _ _ _ (p. 138)

4 Q: Which British pop group's first number one single in the U.K. was called 'Hot Love'?

A: _ _ _ _ _ _ _ _ _ _ _ _ _ _ _ _ (p. 138)

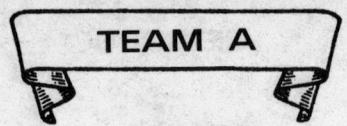

TEAM A

ROUND FIVE
(Team Questions)

1 Q: Which country's naval manoeuvres in
   the summer of 1987, were codenamed
   'Operation Martyrdom'?
   A: _ _ _ _ _ _ _ _ _ _ _ _ _ _ _ _ (p. 141)

     ●

2 Q: What caused a British Army vet to be
   flown out to Gibraltar in August 1987?
   A: _ _ _ _ _ _ _ _ _ _ _ _ _ _ _ _ (p. 141)

     ●

3 Q: A Leonardo Da Vinci cartoon was in the
   news in July 1987. Why?
   A: _ _ _ _ _ _ _ _ _ _ _ _ _ _ _ _ (p. 141)

     ●

4 Q: The 1987 film 'Who's That Girl' was
   slammed by U.S. critics. Who is the
   star of the film?
   A: _ _ _ _ _ _ _ _ _ _ _ _ _ _ _ _ (p. 141)

     ●

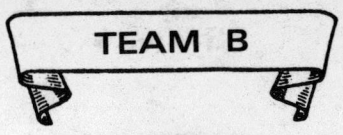

TEAM B

ROUND FIVE
(Team Questions)

---

1 Q: **What nationality was Military Attaché Ivan Djambov ordered out of Britain in July 1987?**

A: _ _ _ _ _ _ _ _ _ _ _ _ _ _ _ _ (p. 144)

───────────●───────────

2 Q: **Which English actress is the leading figure in the Animal Welfare Group 'Zoo Check'?**

A: _ _ _ _ _ _ _ _ _ _ _ _ _ _ _ (p. 144)

───────────●───────────

3 Q: **Which fast-food chain announced in August 1987, that after ten years of negotiations, it would be opening three branches in Russia?**

A: _ _ _ _ _ _ _ _ _ _ _ _ _ _ _ (p. 144)

───────────●───────────

4 Q: **Who is the author of the 1987 book 'Cricket XXXX Cricket'?**

A: _ _ _ _ _ _ _ _ _ _ _ _ _ (p. 144)

───────────●───────────

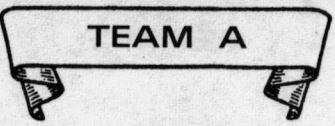

TEAM A

ROUND SIX
(Team Questions)

---

1 Q: What are the very thin high heels of
     women's shoes called?

  A: _ _ _ _ _ _ _ _ _ _ _ _ _ _ _ _ (p. 147)

---

2 Q: The English footballer, Peter Shilton,
     left Leicester City in 1974 to join which
     club?

  A: _ _ _ _ _ _ _ _ _ _ _ _ _ _ _ (p. 147)

---

3 Q: Which 1976 film, starring Robert
     Redford and Dustin Hoffman, dealt
     with the uncovering of the Watergate
     Scandal?

  A: _ _ _ _ _ _ _ _ _ _ _ _ _ _ _ _ (p. 147)

---

4 Q: Which English King died at the Battle of
     Bosworth Field?

  A: _ _ _ _ _ _ _ _ _ _ _ _ _ _ _ (p. 147)

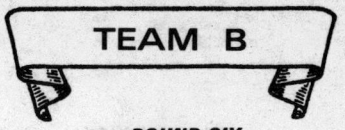

TEAM B

ROUND SIX
(Team Questions)

1 Q: What shape was a traditional 'cocked hat'?

A: _ _ _ _ _ _ _ _ _ _ _ _ _ _ _ _ _ (p. 149)

2 Q: From which English soccer club did Brian Greenhof come before he joined Leeds United?

A: _ _ _ _ _ _ _ _ _ _ _ _ _ _ _ _ _ (p. 149)

3 Q: Which 1969 film about the sleazy side of New York starred Dustin Hoffman and Jon Voight?

A: _ _ _ _ _ _ _ _ _ _ _ _ _ _ _ _ (p. 149)

4 Q: Which English King was defeated at the Battle of Naseby?

A: _ _ _ _ _ _ _ _ _ _ _ _ _ _ _ _ (p. 149)

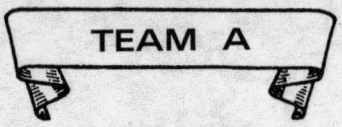

TEAM A

ROUND SEVEN
(Individual Questions: No conferring by either side)

1 Q: Ulan Bator is the capital city of which country?

A: _ _ _ _ _ _ _ _ _ _ _ _ _ _ _ _ (p. 151)

●

2 Q: Who was the girl famous for officiating on the British TV entertainment series the 'Golden Shot'?

A: _ _ _ _ _ _ _ _ _ _ _ _ _ _ _ _ (p. 151)

●

3 Q: For how many years does a British copyright legally last?

A: _ _ _ _ _ _ _ _ _ _ _ _ _ _ _ _ (p. 151)

●

4 Q: Who was born in Norfolk, England in 1737, became connected with rights of man, ranging from slavery to U.S. Independence and died in New York in 1809?

A: _ _ _ _ _ _ _ _ _ _ _ _ _ _ _ _ (p. 151)

●

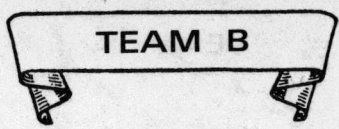

TEAM B

ROUND SEVEN
(Individual Questions: No conferring by either side)

1 Q: By what name was the territory of
Namibia formerly known from 1919
onwards?
A: _ _ _ _ _ _ _ _ _ _ _ _ _ _ _ (p. 153)

●

2 Q: What does Arthur Daley call his wife in
the British TV series 'Minder'?
A: _ _ _ _ _ _ _ _ _ _ _ _ _ _ _ (p. 153)

●

3 Q: What is meant by the literary phrase
'To Bowdlerise'?
A: _ _ _ _ _ _ _ _ _ _ _ _ _ _ _ (p. 153)

●

4 Q: Which French philosopher, playwright
and novelist who died in 1980 was the
leading French exponent of aesthetic
existentialism?
A: _ _ _ _ _ _ _ _ _ _ _ _ _ _ _ (p. 153)

●

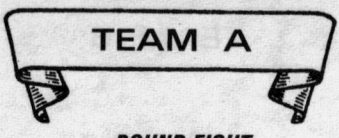

TEAM A

ROUND EIGHT
(Team Questions)

---

1 Q: Burlington House, in London has been
the home of what since 1868?

A: _ _ _ _ _ _ _ _ _ _ _ _ _ _ _ _ _ (p. 156)

---

2 Q: Which member of the clergy would live
in a 'Manse'?

A: _ _ _ _ _ _ _ _ _ _ _ _ _ _ _ _ _ (p. 156)

---

3 Q: Which famous actor was narrator for
the 1963 film 'Zulu' set during Rorke's
Drift battle in 1879?

A: _ _ _ _ _ _ _ _ _ _ _ _ _ _ _ _ (p. 156)

---

4 Q: Name an English county which is
famous for it's Fens, other than
Norfolk?

A: _ _ _ _ _ _ _ _ _ _ _ _ _ _ _ _ _ (p. 156)

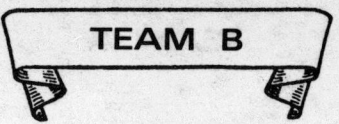

TEAM B

ROUND EIGHT
(Team Questions)

1 Q: In which part of London is the National
     Portrait Gallery located?
   A: _ _ _ _ _ _ _ _ _ _ _ _ _ _ _ _ _ (p. 158)

⬤

2 Q: A 'mercator projection' is most likely to
     be found on what?
   A: _ _ _ _ _ _ _ _ _ _ _ _ _ _ _ _ _ (p. 158)

⬤

3 Q: Which famous actor was narrator for
     the 1962 epic film 'How the West was
     Won'?
   A: _ _ _ _ _ _ _ _ _ _ _ _ _ _ _ _ _ (p. 158)

⬤

4 Q: Ennerdale Water, Crummock and
     Hawes are part of which area in
     England?
   A: _ _ _ _ _ _ _ _ _ _ _ _ _ _ _ _ _ (p. 158)

⬤

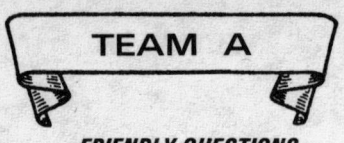

TEAM A

FRIENDLY QUESTIONS

---

1 Q: Which football league team play their home games at Roker Park?

A: _ _ _ _ _ _ _ _ _ _ _ _ _ _ _ _ (p. 162)

---●---

2 Q: What did Mr. Elie Wiesel (vee-ssel) receive at a ceremony at Oslo University in December 1986?

A: _ _ _ _ _ _ _ _ _ _ _ _ _ _ _ _ (p. 162)

---●---

3 Q: In computer terminology, the smallest unit of information is called a bit. How is the word 'bit' derived?

A: _ _ _ _ _ _ _ _ _ _ _ _ _ _ _ _ (p. 162)

---●---

4 Q: What is the stretch of water between Sweden and Denmark called?

A: _ _ _ _ _ _ _ _ _ _ _ _ _ _ _ _ (p. 162)

---●---

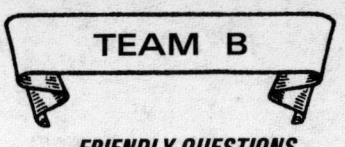

TEAM B

FRIENDLY QUESTIONS

1 Q: Which second division team beat
   Manchester United to win the F.A. Cup
   in 1976?
   A: _ _ _ _ _ _ _ _ _ _ _ _ _ _ _ _ _ (p. 163)

2 Q: The writer of one of the best known
   poems of World War II, 'The Naming of
   Parts', and of many radio plays, died in
   December 1986. Who was he?
   A: _ _ _ _ _ _ _ _ _ _ _ _ _ _ _ _ (p. 163)

3 Q: Many computers process eight bits as
   a single unit known as a byte. What is
   the computer term for half a byte, or
   four bits?
   A: _ _ _ _ _ _ _ _ _ _ _ _ _ _ _ _ _ (p. 163)

4 Q: What is the stretch of water between
   Norway and Denmark called?
   A: _ _ _ _ _ _ _ _ _ _ _ _ _ _ _ _ (p. 163)

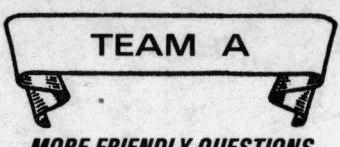

TEAM A

MORE FRIENDLY QUESTIONS

1 Q: The German philosopher Gottfried Leibniz and Isaac Newton independently developed which 17th century innovation in mathematics?

A: _ _ _ _ _ _ _ _ _ _ _ _ _ _ _ _ (p. 162)

2 Q: What was the profession of the acknowledged master, Auguste Escoffier?

A: _ _ _ _ _ _ _ _ _ _ _ _ _ _ _ (p. 162)

3 Q: What sort of things have the following as notable examples, The Great Mogul, The Orlov, and The Jonker?

A: _ _ _ _ _ _ _ _ _ _ _ _ _ _ _ (p. 162)

4 Q: Mr. William Casey collapsed in December 1986 when about to give the U.S. Congress further information about 'Irangate'. What position did he hold?

A: _ _ _ _ _ _ _ _ _ _ _ _ _ _ (p. 162)

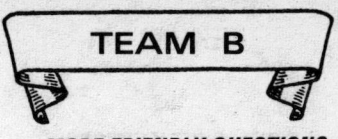

TEAM B

MORE FRIENDLY QUESTIONS

1 Q: Who independently proposed the
    principle of natural selection at the
    same time as Charles Darwin?
  A: _ _ _ _ _ _ _ _ _ _ _ _ _ _ _ _ (p. 163)

2 Q: What was the profession of the
    Frenchman, Emmanuel Poire, who,
    under the pseudonym Caran D'Ache,
    became one of the earliest exponents
    of his art?
  A: _ _ _ _ _ _ _ _ _ _ _ _ _ _ _ _ (p. 163)

3 Q: Which diamond, discovered in 1905,
    was cut to provide the two 'Stars of
    Africa' of the crown jewels?
  A: _ _ _ _ _ _ _ _ _ _ _ _ _ _ _ _ (p. 163)

4 Q: Dr. Davis Wilson was appointed by the
    Queen in January 1987 to be probably
    the last Governor of where?
  A: _ _ _ _ _ _ _ _ _ _ _ _ _ _ _ _ (p. 163)

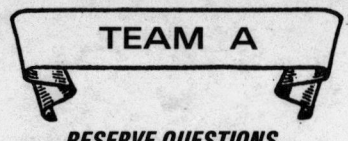

TEAM A

RESERVE QUESTIONS

1 Q: What sport has the Latin name
   of 'Toxophily'?
   A: _ _ _ _ _ _ _ _ _ _ _ _ _ _ _ _ (p. 162)

2 Q: Who lead the Peasant's Revolt in
   1381?
   A: _ _ _ _ _ _ _ _ _ _ _ _ _ _ _ _ (p. 162)

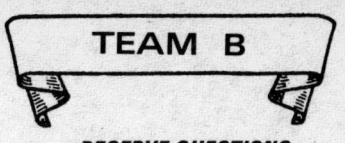

TEAM B

RESERVE QUESTIONS

_____

1 Q: The name of which sport, literally
     translated, means 'Empty Hand'?
   A: _ _ _ _ _ _ _ _ _ _ _ _ _ _ _ _   (p. 163)

_____ ● _____

2 Q: Who led the Fenland Rebellion against
     William I in 1070?
   A: _ _ _ _ _ _ _ _ _ _ _ _ _ _ _ _   (p. 163)

_____ ● _____

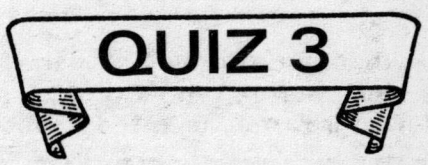

QUIZ 3

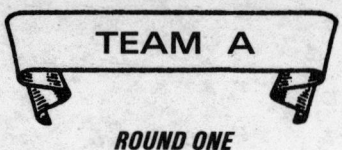

TEAM A

ROUND ONE
(Team Questions)

1 Q: By what name do we know the North
     African country who's Arabic name,
     Al-Maghreb means farthest west?
  A: _ _ _ _ _ _ _ _ _ _ _ _ _ _ _ _ (p. 122)

───────────── ● ─────────────

2 Q: What name is given to the ornamental
     plate around a key hole, which protects
     the surface of the door?
  A: _ _ _ _ _ _ _ _ _ _ _ _ _ (pp. 122–3)

───────────── ● ─────────────

3 Q: Who starred opposite Yul Brynner in
     the 1956 musical film 'The King and I'?
  A: _ _ _ _ _ _ _ _ _ _ _ _ _ _ _ (p. 123)

───────────── ● ─────────────

4 Q: How many numbered slots are there on
     a standard roulette wheel, used in
     gambling?
  A: _ _ _ _ _ _ _ _ _ _ _ _ _ _ _ (p. 123)

───────────── ● ─────────────

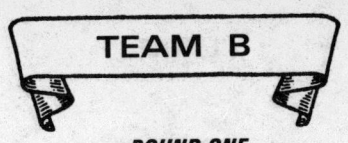

ROUND ONE
(Team Questions)

1 Q: What North African republic is situated
between Algeria to the west and Libya
to the south east?

A: _ _ _ _ _ _ _ _ _ _ _ _ _ _ _ _ (p. 124)

2 Q: In art, what name is given to a pair of
pictures (artworks) hinged together?

A: _ _ _ _ _ _ _ _ _ _ _ _ _ _ _ (p. 125)

3 Q: Kirk Douglas played the wild west
outlaw Doc Holliday in the 1957
western film 'Gunfight at the O.K.
Corral'. Who played Wyatt Earp?

A: _ _ _ _ _ _ _ _ _ _ _ _ _ _ _ (p. 125)

4 Q: On a standard roulette wheel used in
gambling, what colour is the zero slot?

A: _ _ _ _ _ _ _ _ _ _ _ _ _ _ (p. 125)

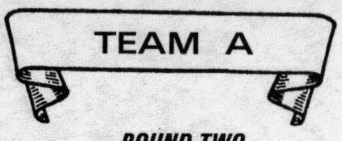

TEAM A

ROUND TWO
(Team Questions)

1 Q: Who was granted the title of Prince of the United Kingdom in 1957?

A: _ _ _ _ _ _ _ _ _ _ _ _ _ _ _ (p. 126)

2 Q: This famous Italian conductor began his career as a cellist, and died in 1957. Who was he?

A: _ _ _ _ _ _ _ _ _ _ _ _ _ _ _ (p. 126)

3 Q: Near which island in the central Pacific, did Britain explode her first H-bomb in 1957?

A: _ _ _ _ _ _ _ _ _ _ _ _ _ _ _ (p. 127)

4 Q: Who resigned as Britain's Prime Minister in January 1957?

A: _ _ _ _ _ _ _ _ _ _ _ _ _ _ _ (p. 127)

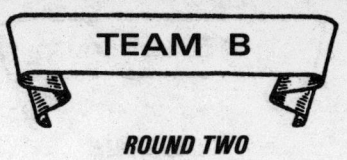

TEAM B

ROUND TWO
(Team Questions)

---

1 Q: What was significant about H.M. the
Queen's 1957 Christmas broadcast?
A: _ _ _ _ _ _ _ _ _ _ _ _ _ _ _ _ (p. 128)

---●---

2 Q: The composer of the symphonic poems
'Kullervo' and 'Finlandia' died in 1957.
Who was he?
A: _ _ _ _ _ _ _ _ _ _ _ _ _ _ _ _ (p. 128)

---●---

3 Q: One of the world's largest radio
telescope was put into operation for
Manchester University in 1957. Where
was it situated?
A: _ _ _ _ _ _ _ _ _ _ _ _ _ _ _ _ (p. 129)

---●---

4 Q: Who was appointed Britain's Prime
Minister in January 1957?
A: _ _ _ _ _ _ _ _ _ _ _ _ _ _ _ _ (p. 129)

---●---

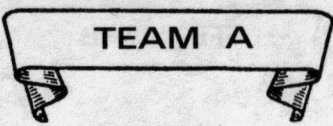

TEAM A

ROUND THREE
(Individual Questions: No conferring by either side)

_____

1 Q: In physics what name is given to the
     study of gases in motion?

   A: _ _ _ _ _ _ _ _ _ _ _ _ _ _ _ _ _ (p. 130)

_____ ● _____

2 Q: What are 'petit pois' (petty pwar) found
     on a menu?

   A: _ _ _ _ _ _ _ _ _ _ _ _ _ _ _ _ _ (p. 130)

_____ ● _____

3 Q: Which English girl won both the one
     hundred metres and two hundred
     metres in the 1962 Commonwealth
     Games?

   A: _ _ _ _ _ _ _ _ _ _ _ _ _ _ _ _ (p. 131)

_____ ● _____

4 Q: Why was the former Cabinet Minister
     James Prior so upset in December
     1986 when the government decided
     not to buy the GEC Nimrod airborne
     warning system?

   A: _ _ _ _ _ _ _ _ _ _ _ _ _ _ _ _ (p. 131)

_____ ● _____

_____

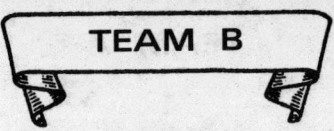

TEAM B

ROUND THREE
(Individual Questions: No conferring by either side)

1 Q: In chemistry what name is given to the
     suspension of a liquid in a gas?
   A: _ _ _ _ _ _ _ _ _ _ _ _ _ _ _ _   (p. 132)

●

2 Q: What does the french word 'coq'
     (cock) refer to on a menu?
   A: _ _ _ _ _ _ _ _ _ _ _ _ _ _ _ _ _   (p. 133)

●

3 Q: Who won the shot putt for Britain in
     the Commonwealth Games of 1974
     and 1978?
   A: _ _ _ _ _ _ _ _ _ _ _ _ _ _ _ _ _   (p. 133)

●

4 Q: What type of aircraft will the RAF
     continue to use for airborne radar cover
     until the arrival of the AWACS system
     in 1991?
   A: _ _ _ _ _ _ _ _ _ _ _ _ _ _ _ _ _   (p. 133)

●

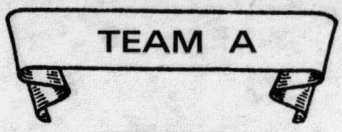

TEAM A

ROUND FOUR
(Team Questions)

1 Q: Who was the composer of the 'Bear Symphony' in 1786?
   A: _ _ _ _ _ _ _ _ _ _ _ _ _ _ _ _ _ (p. 136)

———————————— ● ————————————

2 Q: What are culottes?
   A: _ _ _ _ _ _ _ _ _ _ _ _ _ _ _ _ _ (p. 136)

———————————— ● ————————————

3 Q: In which novel does the middle-aged Jewish musician 'Svengali' appear?
   A: _ _ _ _ _ _ _ _ _ _ _ _ _ _ _ _ _ (p. 136)

———————————— ● ————————————

4 Q: In which film did Tony Curtis and Jack Lemon both disguise themselves as girl musicians?
   A: _ _ _ _ _ _ _ _ _ _ _ _ _ _ _ _ _ (p. 136)

———————————— ● ————————————

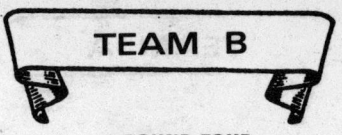

TEAM B

ROUND FOUR
(Team Questions)

1 Q: Which composer told in music the story of an afternoon in the life of a fawn in 1894?

A: _ _ _ _ _ _ _ _ _ _ _ _ _ _ _ _ (p. 139)

2 Q: From what source does Castor Oil come?

A: _ _ _ _ _ _ _ _ _ _ _ _ _ _ _ _ (p. 139)

3 Q: In Greek legend Penelope was the wife of whom?

A: _ _ _ _ _ _ _ _ _ _ _ _ _ _ _ _ (p. 139)

4 Q: Who starred as country singer Loretta Lynn in the 1980 film 'Coal Miner's Daughter'?

A: _ _ _ _ _ _ _ _ _ _ _ _ _ _ _ (p. 139)

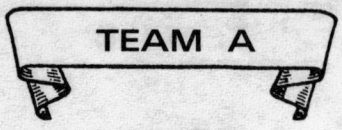

TEAM A

ROUND FIVE
(Team Questions)

1 Q: What do Americans Jim and Tammy
     Bakker and Jerry Falwell have in
     common?
  A: _ _ _ _ _ _ _ _ _ _ _ _ _ _ _ (p. 141)

_____ ● _____

2 Q: Which former Labour MP, in August
     1987, denied allegations that he had
     been a Czech, spy?
  A: _ _ _ _ _ _ _ _ _ _ _ _ _ _ _ (p. 142)

_____ ● _____

3 Q: What was unusual about the return of
     Poppy, a lost budgerigar, to her Bristol
     owner in August 1987?
  A: _ _ _ _ _ _ _ _ _ _ _ _ _ _ _ (p. 142)

_____ ● _____

4 Q: The 10th anniversary of whose death
     was celebrated with documentaries
     and films on T.V. during the summer of
     1987?
  A: _ _ _ _ _ _ _ _ _ _ _ _ _ _ _ _ (p. 142)

_____ ● _____

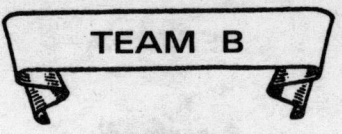

TEAM B

ROUND FIVE
(Team Questions)

1 Q: Which comedian was banned from driving for three years in August 1987, after inviting a policeman to 'nick' him after he had been drinking?

A: _ _ _ _ _ _ _ _ _ _ _ _ _ _ _ _ (p. 144)

2 Q: A Chairman of the Lonrho business group, he is a former Chairman of the Conservative party. Name him.

A: _ _ _ _ _ _ _ _ _ _ _ _ _ _ _ _ (p. 145)

3 Q: American Jim Dickson began an attempted crossing of the Atlantic in August 1987. What made his attempt unusual?

A: _ _ _ _ _ _ _ _ _ _ _ _ _ _ _ (p. 145)

4 Q: Complete the title of the 1987 feature length cartoon 'Pinocchio and the. . . . .?

A: _ _ _ _ _ _ _ _ _ _ _ _ _ _ _ (p. 145)

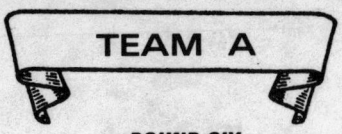

TEAM A

ROUND SIX
(Team Questions)

1 Q: The assassination of Archduke Ferdinand of Austria, set off a chain of events which led to what?

A: _ _ _ _ _ _ _ _ _ _ _ _ _ _ _ (p. 147)

2 Q: Which composer wrote the music for the ballet 'Billy the Kid' in 1938?

A: _ _ _ _ _ _ _ _ _ _ _ _ _ _ _ (p. 147)

3 Q: In which film did Roger Moore make his debut as James Bond?

A: _ _ _ _ _ _ _ _ _ _ _ _ _ _ _ (p. 148)

4 Q: Near which town in England is Anne Hathaway's cottage?

A: _ _ _ _ _ _ _ _ _ _ _ _ _ _ _ (p. 148)

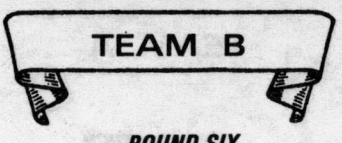

TEAM B

ROUND SIX
(Team Questions)

_____

1 Q: What is the children's rhyme 'Ring-a
   Ring-o-Roses' thought to refer to?
   A: _ _ _ _ _ _ _ _ _ _ _ _ _ _ _ _ (p. 149)

   ─────────────●─────────────

2 Q: Which composer wrote the opera 'Billy
   Budd' in 1951?
   A: _ _ _ _ _ _ _ _ _ _ _ _ _ _ _ _ (p. 149)

   ─────────────●─────────────

3 Q: Whose film breakthrough came with
   his portrayal of a drunken young lawyer
   in the film 'Easy Rider'?
   A: _ _ _ _ _ _ _ _ _ _ _ _ _ _ _ _ (p. 150)

   ─────────────●─────────────

4 Q: In which English county is the
   Glyndebourne Opera House located, at
   which an annual festival is held?
   A: _ _ _ _ _ _ _ _ _ _ _ _ _ _ _ _ (p. 150)

   ─────────────●─────────────

   _____

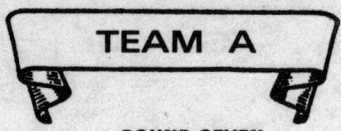

TEAM A

ROUND SEVEN
(Individual Questions: No conferring by either side)

1 Q: **What was the Russian assembly (parliament) called before the Revolution of 1917?**

   A: _ _ _ _ _ _ _ _ _ _ _ _ _ _ _ _ (p. 151)

   ———————●———————

2 Q: **Which racehorse trainer set a postwar Royal Ascot record with seven winners in June 1987?**

   A: _ _ _ _ _ _ _ _ _ _ _ _ _ _ _ _ (p. 152)

   ———————●———————

3 Q: **What is the most common tuberous-rooted food crop of this country?**

   A: _ _ _ _ _ _ _ _ _ _ _ _ _ _ _ (p. 152)

   ———————●———————

4 Q: **What is the primary concern of a member of the Howard League in Britain?**

   A: _ _ _ _ _ _ _ _ _ _ _ _ _ _ _ (p. 152)

   ———————●———————

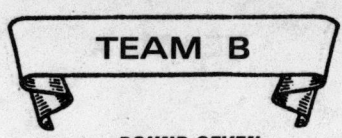

TEAM B

ROUND SEVEN
(Individual Questions: No conferring by either side)

1 Q: What was the 'Balfour Declaration' of
    1917?
   A: _ _ _ _ _ _ _ _ _ _ _ _ _ _ _ _ (p. 154)

2 Q: Which jockey rode a record eight
    winners at Royal Ascot in 1965 and
    again in 1975?
   A: _ _ _ _ _ _ _ _ _ _ _ _ _ _ _ _ (p. 154)

3 Q: Laver and Dulse are edible types of
    which plant?
   A: _ _ _ _ _ _ _ _ _ _ _ _ _ _ _ _ (p. 154)

4 Q: 'Carthusians' are the old boys from
    which public school in England?
   A: _ _ _ _ _ _ _ _ _ _ _ _ _ _ _ (p. 154)

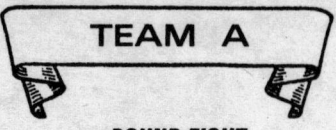

TEAM A

ROUND EIGHT
(Team Questions)

1 Q: From what is 'semolina', used in milk
     pudding desserts made?
   A: _ _ _ _ _ _ _ _ _ _ _ _ _ _ _ _   (p. 156)

2 Q: What was the name of the Roman god
     of sleep which is perpetuated in an
     English word meaning sleepy or
     drowsy?
   A: _ _ _ _ _ _ _ _ _ _ _ _ _ _ _ _   (p. 156)

3 Q: What regulating body is represented by
     the letters B.B.B.C. in Britain?
   A: _ _ _ _ _ _ _ _ _ _ _ _ _ _ _ _   (p. 157)

4 Q: What famous London landmark is
     topped by a seventeen feet high statue
     sculptured by E.H. Baily?
   A: _ _ _ _ _ _ _ _ _ _ _ _ _ _ _ _   (p. 157)

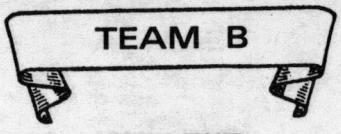

TEAM B

ROUND EIGHT
(Team Questions)

1 Q: What is sago, as used in milk pudding
   desserts?
   A: _ _ _ _ _ _ _ _ _ _ _ _ _ _ _ _   (p. 158)

---●---

2 Q: In which country of the world would
   you find adherents of the ancient
   'Coptic Church'?
   A: _ _ _ _ _ _ _ _ _ _ _ _ _ _ _ _   (p. 159)

---●---

3 Q: What regulating body is represented by
   the letters B.B.F.C. in Britain?
   A: _ _ _ _ _ _ _ _ _ _ _ _ _ _ _ _   (p. 159)

---●---

4 Q: Who re-built the Brighton Pavilion from
   1815—1823?
   A: _ _ _ _ _ _ _ _ _ _ _ _ _ _ _ _   (p. 159)

---●---

INTERESTING FACT:
*The Beeston Castle in Beestone was once owned by Lord Tollemache
and he used to have his trains stop outside so that travellers could
enjoy refreshment.*

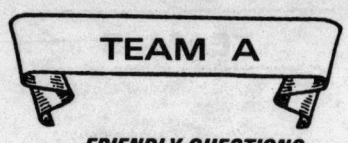

FRIENDLY QUESTIONS

---

1 Q: How many sisters complete the name
of the well known North London Road?

   A: _ _ _ _ _ _ _ _ _ _ _ _ _ _ _ _ (p. 164)

---

2 Q: In which 1978 BBC TV series did the
characters Anna Newcross, Sarah
Lloyd-Smith and Jay Harper feature?

   A: _ _ _ _ _ _ _ _ _ _ _ _ _ _ _ _ (p. 164)

---

3 Q: If your 24 hour clock was 35 minutes
slow and showed the time as 1750
hours, how long would you have, to
keep an appointment at 6.30 p.m.?

   A: _ _ _ _ _ _ _ _ _ _ _ _ _ _ _ _ (p. 164)

---

4 Q: Which fictional bear was the hero of a
book by Richard Adams?

   A: _ _ _ _ _ _ _ _ _ _ _ _ _ _ _ _ (p. 164)

TEAM B

FRIENDLY QUESTIONS

1 Q: Give the colloquial name of London's
Middlesex Street, site of a popular
market?

A: _ _ _ _ _ _ _ _ _ _ _ _ _ _ _ _ _ (p. 165)

2 Q: Who is the actress who originally
played the mother 'that makes three' in
the BBC TV comedy series of the 70s?

A: _ _ _ _ _ _ _ _ _ _ _ _ _ _ _ _ _ (p. 165)

3 Q: If you paid two hundred and thirty
pounds for an item that included 15%
V.A.T. how much would the same
thing have cost without V.A.T.?

A: _ _ _ _ _ _ _ _ _ _ _ _ _ _ _ _ _ (p. 165)

4 Q: Which author wrote the novel 'De la
terre a la lune' (in which he stated that
Cape Kennedy would be used for
shooting a capsule to the moon)?

A: _ _ _ _ _ _ _ _ _ _ _ _ _ _ _ _ _ (p. 165)

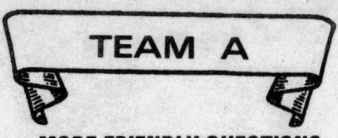

TEAM A

MORE FRIENDLY QUESTIONS

---

1 Q: If you were in a French restaurant and ordered 'pommes de terre frites' what would you get?

A: _ _ _ _ _ _ _ _ _ _ _ _ _ _ _ _ (p. 164)

———————————————•———————————————

2 Q: Apart from being names, 'Gilbert', 'Marshall', 'Solomon', 'Caroline' and 'Mariana', are all types of what?

A: _ _ _ _ _ _ _ _ _ _ _ _ _ _ _ _ (p. 164)

———————————————•———————————————

3 Q: Which American film actor has starred in the films 'M.A.S.H.' (1970), 'Klute' (1971), and 'Don't Look Now' (1973)?

A: _ _ _ _ _ _ _ _ _ _ _ _ _ _ _ _ (p. 164)

———————————————•———————————————

4 Q: What type of musical instrument is a 'Marimba'?

A: _ _ _ _ _ _ _ _ _ _ _ _ _ _ _ _ (p. 164)

———————————————•———————————————

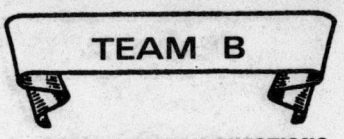

MORE FRIENDLY QUESTIONS

---

1 Q: What kind of food is the French dish vichyssoise (vee-see-swah)?

A: _ _ _ _ _ _ _ _ _ _ _ _ _ _ _ _   (p. 165)

●

---

2 Q: One word signifies the following: a military weapon, a type of cement, an article used by a chemist. What is the word?

A: _ _ _ _ _ _ _ _ _ _ _ _ _ _ _ _ _   (p. 165)

●

---

3 Q: Which American film actor has starred in the films 'Kotch' (1971), 'Charley Varrick' (1973), and 'The Sunshine Boys' (1975)?

A: _ _ _ _ _ _ _ _ _ _ _ _ _ _ _ _   (p. 165)

●

---

4 Q: On which musical instrument would you be most likely to play a 'pibroch' (pea-brock)?

A: _ _ _ _ _ _ _ _ _ _ _ _ _ _ _ _ _   (p. 165)

●

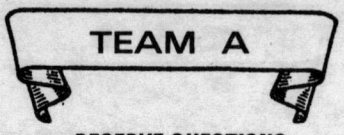

TEAM A

RESERVE QUESTIONS

---

1 Q: In which Polish city is the second
       oldest university in Central Europe,
       where the astronomer Copernicus was
       a student?
   A: _ _ _ _ _ _ _ _ _ _ _ _ _ _ _ _   (p. 164)

─────────────────── ● ───────────────────

2 Q: Who recorded the song 'Little Arrows'
       in 1968?
   A: _ _ _ _ _ _ _ _ _ _ _ _ _ _ _   (p. 164)

─────────────────── ● ───────────────────

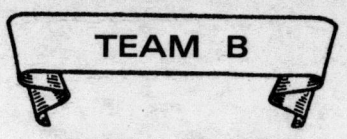

TEAM B

RESERVE QUESTIONS

---

1 Q: What is the name of the game reserve in North East Transvaal, South Africa, situated between the Limpopo river and Komatipoort?

  A: _ _ _ _ _ _ _ _ _ _ _ _ _ _ _ _ (p. 165)

---

2 Q: Who recorded the song 'Little Children' in 1964?

  A: _ _ _ _ _ _ _ _ _ _ _ _ _ _ _ (p. 165)

QUIZ 4

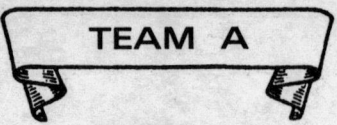

TEAM A

ROUND ONE
(Team Questions)

1 Q: When crossing the International Date
     Line, what happens to the date when
     travelling from West to East?
  A: _ _ _ _ _ _ _ _ _ _ _ _ _ _ _ _ _ _ (p. 123)

●

2 Q: In which country was former U.S.
     Secretary of State, Henry Kissinger
     born?
  A: _ _ _ _ _ _ _ _ _ _ _ _ _ _ _ _ _ _ (p. 123)

●

3 Q: What is a 'turbo-prop' aeroplane?
  A: _ _ _ _ _ _ _ _ _ _ _ _ _ _ _ _ _ _ (p. 123)

●

4 Q: What Essex-born author wrote the
     novel 'The French Lieutenant's
     Woman' and a philosophical study
     called 'The Aristos'?
  A: _ _ _ _ _ _ _ _ _ _ _ _ _ _ _ _ _ _ (p. 123)

●

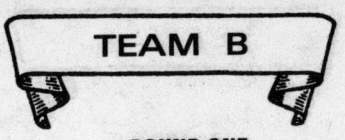

TEAM B

ROUND ONE
(Team Questions)

---

1 Q: Which European explorer discovered
   Lake Victoria which was believed to be
   the source of the River Nile?
   A: _ _ _ _ _ _ _ _ _ _ _ _ _ _ _ _ (p. 125)

---•---

2 Q: In which country was the mountaineer
   and explorer Sir Edmund Hillary, who
   climbed Mount Everest, born?
   A: _ _ _ _ _ _ _ _ _ _ _ _ _ _ _ _ (p. 125)

---•---

3 Q: What was a 'flying-boat'?
   A: _ _ _ _ _ _ _ _ _ _ _ _ _ _ _ _ (p. 125)

---•---

4 Q: Name the American who was a leading
   man in many 1940s films, and
   published his autobiography in 1965
   called 'Where's the Rest of Me'?
   A: _ _ _ _ _ _ _ _ _ _ _ _ _ _ _ _ (p. 125)

---•---

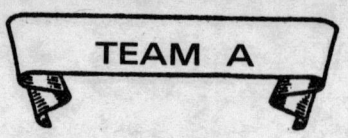

ROUND TWO
(Team Questions)

---

1 Q: In August 1965 what product was banned from advertising in TV commercials in Britain?

A: _ _ _ _ _ _ _ _ _ _ _ _ _ _ _ _ (p. 127)

---•---

2 Q: Name the Egyptian ex-king died in March 1965 aged forty-five.

A: _ _ _ _ _ _ _ _ _ _ _ _ _ _ _ _ (p. 127)

---•---

3 Q: In, 1965, Karen Muir set up a women's sporting record aged only twelve years. Which sport?

A: _ _ _ _ _ _ _ _ _ _ _ _ _ _ _ _ (p. 127)

---•---

4 Q: In May 1965 Franz Jonas was elected president of which country in Europe?

A: _ _ _ _ _ _ _ _ _ _ _ _ _ _ _ _ (p. 127)

---•---

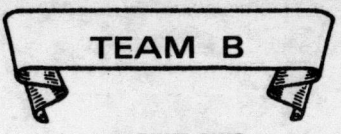

TEAM B

ROUND TWO
(Team Questions)

1 Q: Name the most popular offshore pirate
     commercial radio station which was
     established in 1965 close to Britain.
   A: _ _ _ _ _ _ _ _ _ _ _ _ _ _ _ _   (p. 129)

●

2 Q: Name the musical "King" who died in
     February 1965, at the age of forty five.
   A: _ _ _ _ _ _ _ _ _ _ _ _ _ _ _ _ _   (p. 129)

●

3 Q: In July 1965, Madame Vaucher
     became the first woman to achieve
     what sporting accomplishment?
   A: _ _ _ _ _ _ _ _ _ _ _ _ _ _ _ _   (p. 129)

●

4 Q: Name the Black Muslim leader who
     was shot dead in Manhattan, USA, in
     February 1965.
   A: _ _ _ _ _ _ _ _ _ _ _ _ _ _ _ _   (p. 129)

●

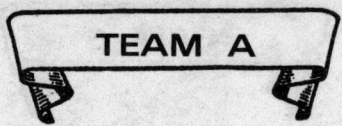

TEAM A

ROUND THREE
(Individual Questions: No conferring by either side)

1 Q: Give the name of Sweden's parliament
   A: _ _ _ _ _ _ _ _ _ _ _ _ _ _ _ _ (p. 131)

   ──────────── ● ────────────

2 Q: Which American novelist wrote *A Portrait of a Lady?*
   A: _ _ _ _ _ _ _ _ _ _ _ _ _ _ _ _ (p. 131)

   ──────────── ● ────────────

3 Q: Under which sign of the Zodiac is a birthday on 5th November?
   A: _ _ _ _ _ _ _ _ _ _ _ _ _ _ _ _ (p. 131)

   ──────────── ● ────────────

4 Q: Name the Emperor of Japan during the second World War.
   A: _ _ _ _ _ _ _ _ _ _ _ _ _ _ _ _ (p. 131)

   ──────────── ● ────────────

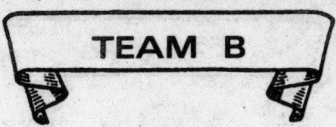

TEAM B

ROUND THREE
(Individual Questions: No conferring by either side)

1 Q: In which country is the port of
Europoort?
A: _ _ _ _ _ _ _ _ _ _ _ _ _ _ _ _ _ (p. 133)

●

2 Q: Which novelist and playwright wrote
The Picture of Dorian Grey?
A: _ _ _ _ _ _ _ _ _ _ _ _ _ _ _ _ (p. 133)

●

3 Q: Under which sign of the Zodiac is a
birthday on 25th December?
A: _ _ _ _ _ _ _ _ _ _ _ _ _ _ _ _ (p. 133)

●

4 Q: In 1944 paratroops were dropped on a
Dutch town as part of an Allied plan to
shorten the second World War, but the
plan ended in disaster. Name the town.
A: _ _ _ _ _ _ _ _ _ _ _ _ _ _ _ _ _ (p. 133)

●

INTERESTING FACT:
A nun in a grey habit is said to haunt the Angel Inn in Catterick.

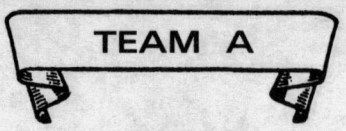

ROUND FOUR
(Team Questions)

1 Q: Which former Duke of Bohemia is well
     known to us through Christmas Carols?
   A: _ _ _ _ _ _ _ _ _ _ _ _ _ _ _ _ (p. 136)

—————————————— ● ——————————————

2 Q: Who was the Biblical Old Testament
     David, King of the Hebrew's son?
   A: _ _ _ _ _ _ _ _ _ _ _ _ _ _ _ _ (p. 136)

—————————————— ● ——————————————

3 Q: Which American actor said of himself,
     'I have eyes like those of a dead pig'?
   A: _ _ _ _ _ _ _ _ _ _ _ _ _ _ _ _ (p. 136)

—————————————— ● ——————————————

4 Q: Who was the youngest soccer player
     to first score 100 goals in the English
     football league?
   A: _ _ _ _ _ _ _ _ _ _ _ _ _ _ _ _ _ (p. 136)

—————————————— ● ——————————————

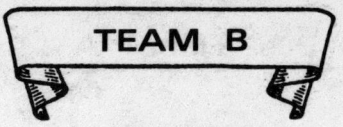

TEAM B

ROUND FOUR
(Team Questions)

1 Q: What was the name of the girl featured
   in the stories of Robin Hood?
   A: _ _ _ _ _ _ _ _ _ _ _ _ _ _ _ (p. 139)

   ●

2 Q: What name is given to the monk in
   charge of an abbey in the Catholic
   church?
   A: _ _ _ _ _ _ _ _ _ _ _ _ _ _ _ (p. 139)

   ●

3 Q: Who painted a famous self-portrait in
   1745 entitled 'Self Portrait with Dog'?
   A: _ _ _ _ _ _ _ _ _ _ _ _ _ _ _ (p. 139)

   ●

4 Q: Who was Fulham's most capped
   International soccer player; from
   1954–62?
   A: _ _ _ _ _ _ _ _ _ _ _ _ _ _ _ (p. 139)

   ●

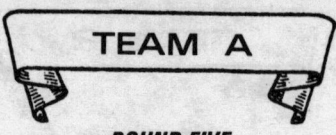

TEAM A

ROUND FIVE
(Team Questions)

1 Q: Actress Michelle Dotrice is married to
   the star of the T.V. series 'The
   Equalizer'. Who is he?
   A: _ _ _ _ _ _ _ _ _ _ _ _ _ _ _ _   (p. 142)

───────────── ● ─────────────

2 Q: Which journey, first taken in 1787, did
   the square-rigged sailing ship 'Young
   Endeavour' begin in July 1987?
   A: _ _ _ _ _ _ _ _ _ _ _ _ _ _ _ _   (p. 142)

───────────── ● ─────────────

3 Q: At which research centre did British
   servicemen allege, in July 1987, that
   they had suffered injuries in lethal nerve
   gas tests?
   A: _ _ _ _ _ _ _ _ _ _ _ _ _ _ _ _   (p. 142)

───────────── ● ─────────────

4 Q: Which American sportswear firm did
   the remaining Beatles decide to sue, in
   July 1987, for unauthorised use of one
   of their recordings in an advert?
   A: _ _ _ _ _ _ _ _ _ _ _ _ _ _ _ _   (p. 142)

───────────── ● ─────────────

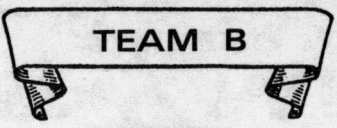

TEAM B

ROUND FIVE
(Team Questions)

1 Q: In which T.V. series shown on Channel
4, did Ed Asner star as the editor of the
Los Angeles Tribune?

A: _ _ _ _ _ _ _ _ _ _ _ _ _ _ _ _   (p. 145)

————————————●————————————

2 Q: What did Concorde smash in a record
breaking time of 103 minutes in July
1987?

A: _ _ _ _ _ _ _ _ _ _ _ _ _ _ _ _   (p. 145)

————————————●————————————

3 Q: Why were Soviet workers Viktor
Bryukhanov, Nikolai Fomin and Anatoly
Dyatlov all gaoled in July 1987?

A: _ _ _ _ _ _ _ _ _ _ _ _ _ _ _ _   (p. 145)

————————————●————————————

4 Q: Which product was advertised, for the
first time ever on Britain's T.V. screens,
on 1st August, 1987?

A: _ _ _ _ _ _ _ _ _ _ _ _ _ _ _ _   (p. 145)

————————————●————————————

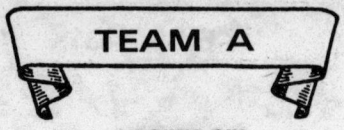

TEAM A

ROUND SIX
(Team Questions)

---

1 Q: The first open tennis tournament in the world, with pro players as well as amateurs, was held in Britain in 1968. In which town?

A: _ _ _ _ _ _ _ _ _ _ _ _ _ _ _ _ **(p. 148)**

---●---

2 Q: How did Mrs. Davina Thompson make medical history in December 1986?

A: _ _ _ _ _ _ _ _ _ _ _ _ _ _ _ _ **(p. 148)**

---●---

3 Q: What is the capital town of the Scilly Isles, on St. Mary's Isle?

A: _ _ _ _ _ _ _ _ _ _ _ _ _ _ _ _ **(p. 148)**

---●---

4 Q: Which explorer sailed in a ship called the 'Santa Maria'?

A: _ _ _ _ _ _ _ _ _ _ _ _ _ _ _ _ **(p. 148)**

---●---

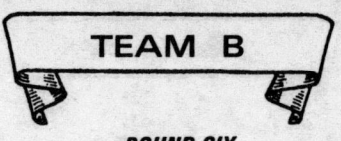

ROUND SIX
(Team Questions)

1 Q: Which tennis player won both the
     American and Wimbledon mens singles
     finals in 1955 without dropping a single
     set?
   A: _ _ _ _ _ _ _ _ _ _ _ _ _ _ _ _ (p. 150)

   ●

2 Q: Which anniversary was celebrated by
     Esperanto speakers in 1987?
   A: _ _ _ _ _ _ _ _ _ _ _ _ _ _ _ _ (p. 150)

   ●

3 Q: In which Swiss town was the
     International Red Cross Society
     established in 1864?
   A: _ _ _ _ _ _ _ _ _ _ _ _ _ _ _ _ (p. 150)

   ●

4 Q: Which well known person sailed in a
     ship called the 'Terra Nova'?
   A: _ _ _ _ _ _ _ _ _ _ _ _ _ _ _ _ (p. 150)

   ●

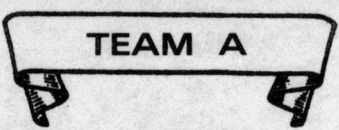

TEAM A

ROUND SEVEN
(Individual Questions: No conferring by either side)

1 Q: When a pestle (pest-l) and mortar are
   used in a laboratory, for what purpose
   is the pestle used?
   A: _ _ _ _ _ _ _ _ _ _ _ _ _ _ _ _ (p. 152)

   ———————————— ● ————————————

2 Q: Which Briton won the World Motor
   Racing Championship in 1976?
   A: _ _ _ _ _ _ _ _ _ _ _ _ _ _ _ _ (p. 152)

   ———————————— ● ————————————

3 Q: Which king founded the Royal
   Academy (of Arts) in London?
   A: _ _ _ _ _ _ _ _ _ _ _ _ _ _ _ _ (p. 152)

   ———————————— ● ————————————

4 Q: In the opera, 'Madame Butterfly' by
   Puccini, the tenor Pinkerton is a
   lieutenant in what navy?
   A: _ _ _ _ _ _ _ _ _ _ _ _ _ _ _ _ (p. 152)

   ———————————— ● ————————————

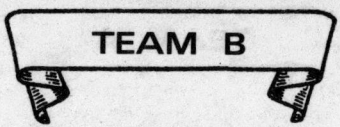

TEAM B

ROUND SEVEN
(Individual Questions: No conferring by either side)

1 Q: What is a better known name for
   phenol (fee-nol), a powerful antiseptic
   and strong disinfectant?
   A: _ _ _ _ _ _ _ _ _ _ _ _ _ _ _ _ (p. 154)

---●---

2 Q: What was the nationality of 1979
   World Racing Champion Jody
   Scheckter?
   A: _ _ _ _ _ _ _ _ _ _ _ _ _ _ _ _ (p. 154)

---●---

3 Q: Who designed the Royal Hospital,
   Chelsea, London?
   A: _ _ _ _ _ _ _ _ _ _ _ _ _ _ _ _ (p. 154)

---●---

4 Q: What type of role was the English
   stage actress Sarah Siddons famous
   for portraying?
   A: _ _ _ _ _ _ _ _ _ _ _ _ _ _ _ _ (p. 154)

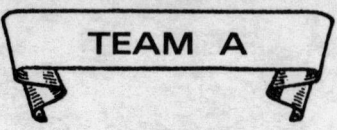

ROUND EIGHT
(Team Questions)

---

1 Q: What city is co-extensive with the
    District of Colombia in the U.S.A.?
  A: _ _ _ _ _ _ _ _ _ _ _ _ _ _ _ _ (p. 157)

━━━━━━━━━━━━━ ● ━━━━━━━━━━━━━

2 Q: What is meant by a persons 'alter ego'?
  A: _ _ _ _ _ _ _ _ _ _ _ _ _ _ _ _ (p. 157)

━━━━━━━━━━━━━ ● ━━━━━━━━━━━━━

3 Q: Which actor starred in the 1971 film
    'Get Carter'?
  A: _ _ _ _ _ _ _ _ _ _ _ _ _ _ _ _ (p. 157)

━━━━━━━━━━━━━ ● ━━━━━━━━━━━━━

4 Q: Name the large bottle in which
    Champagne is sold that is equal to
    twenty bottles?
  A: _ _ _ _ _ _ _ _ _ _ _ _ _ _ _ _ (p. 157)

━━━━━━━━━━━━━ ● ━━━━━━━━━━━━━

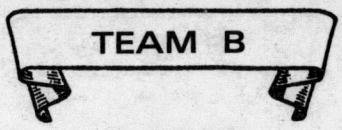

TEAM B

ROUND EIGHT
(Team Questions)

1 Q: What is the capital of the state of
Hawaii, in the U.S.A.?
A: _ _ _ _ _ _ _ _ _ _ _ _ _ _ _ (p. 159)

●

2 Q: What is meant by a 'sequestered' life?
A: _ _ _ _ _ _ _ _ _ _ _ _ _ _ _ (p. 159)

●

3 Q: Which actor starred in the 1958
comedy film 'Lucky Jim'?
A: _ _ _ _ _ _ _ _ _ _ _ _ _ _ _ (p. 159)

●

4 Q: What value has the number described
as a googol in mathematics?
A: _ _ _ _ _ _ _ _ _ _ _ _ _ _ _ (p. 159)

●

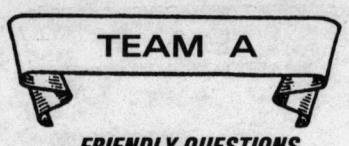

FRIENDLY QUESTIONS

1 Q: What is a person described as an apostate?

A: _ _ _ _ _ _ _ _ _ _ _ _ _ _ _ _ (p. 166)

2 Q: What does a gallon of water weigh, in pounds?

A: _ _ _ _ _ _ _ _ _ _ _ _ _ _ _ _ (p. 166)

3 Q: Which island are the Grand Banks Fishing grounds nearest to?

A: _ _ _ _ _ _ _ _ _ _ _ _ _ _ _ _ (p. 166)

4 Q: Complete the following well known proverb: 'Don't hide your light. . . . .'?

A: _ _ _ _ _ _ _ _ _ _ _ _ _ _ _ _ (p. 166)

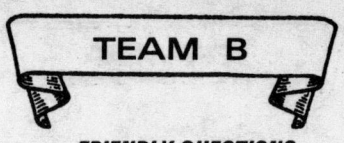

TEAM B

FRIENDLY QUESTIONS

---

1 Q: What is a person described as a proselyte (prossy-lite)?

A: _ _ _ _ _ _ _ _ _ _ _ _ _ _ _ _ _ (p. 167)

---

2 Q: What is the equivalent temperature in degrees Fahrenheit of 100 degrees centigrade?

A: _ _ _ _ _ _ _ _ _ _ _ _ _ _ _ _ (p. 167)

---

3 Q: In which country is the city of Sao Paulo?

A: _ _ _ _ _ _ _ _ _ _ _ _ _ _ _ _ _ (p. 167)

---

4 Q: Complete the following well known proverb: 'To kill the goose that laid. . . . .'?

A: _ _ _ _ _ _ _ _ _ _ _ _ _ _ _ _ (p. 167)

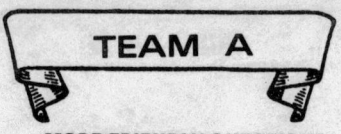

TEAM   A

MORE FRIENDLY QUESTIONS

---

1 Q: What is a 'whetstone' used for
   primarily?
   A: _ _ _ _ _ _ _ _ _ _ _ _ _ _ _ _ (p. 166)

———————————— • ————————————

2 Q: In which American state would you
   find the town of San Diego?
   A: _ _ _ _ _ _ _ _ _ _ _ _ _ _ _ _ (p. 166)

———————————— • ————————————

3 Q: Who was the author of the romantic
   novel, 'The Master of Ballantrae'?
   A: _ _ _ _ _ _ _ _ _ _ _ _ _ _ _ _ (p. 166)

4 Q: In which Mozart opera does the High
   Priest Sarasto address the aria 'O Isis
   and Osiris' to the Ancient Egyptian
   Gods?
   A: _ _ _ _ _ _ _ _ _ _ _ _ _ _ _ _ (p. 166)

———————————— • ————————————

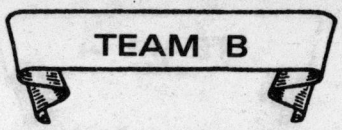

TEAM B

MORE FRIENDLY QUESTIONS

---

1 Q: What was a name given to the coal
　　wagons immediately attached to steam
　　railway engines?

　A: _ _ _ _ _ _ _ _ _ _ _ _ _ _ _ _ _ (p. 167)

———————————— ● ————————————

2 Q: Who planned the American city of
　　Philadelphia in the 1680s?

　A: _ _ _ _ _ _ _ _ _ _ _ _ _ _ _ _ _ (p. 167)

———————————— ● ————————————

3 Q: Name the novel written by Alan Sillitoe,
　　in 1959 about a boy in a Borstal.

　A: _ _ _ _ _ _ _ _ _ _ _ _ _ _ _ _ _ (p. 167)

———————————— ● ————————————

4 Q: Which was Wagner's last opera in
　　1881 that includes the 'Good Friday
　　Music'?

　A: _ _ _ _ _ _ _ _ _ _ _ _ _ _ _ _ _ (p. 167)

———————————— ● ————————————

———————————————————

INTERESTING FACT:
*The actor Charles Laughton was born in the Victoria Hotel in
Scarborough.*

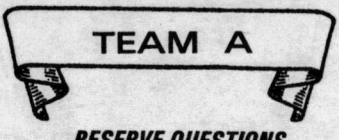

TEAM A

RESERVE QUESTIONS

1 Q: What is the name of the international daily newspaper of the religious group, The Christian Scientists?

A: _ _ _ _ _ _ _ _ _ _ _ _ _ _ _ _ (p. 166)

———————●———————

2 Q: What is the original name given to the art of applying cut out designs and patterned materials to any surface to create an attractive pattern?

A: _ _ _ _ _ _ _ _ _ _ _ _ _ _ _ _ (p. 166)

———————●———————

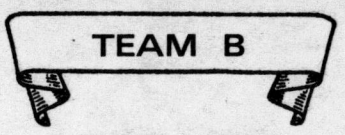

TEAM B

RESERVE QUESTIONS

1 Q: What is the official publication of the religious group the Jehovah's Witnesses?

A: _ _ _ _ _ _ _ _ _ _ _ _ _ _ _ (p. 167)

2 Q: What is the name given to the art of decorating or engraving the bones and ivory of whales and walruses?

A: _ _ _ _ _ _ _ _ _ _ _ _ _ _ _ (p. 167)

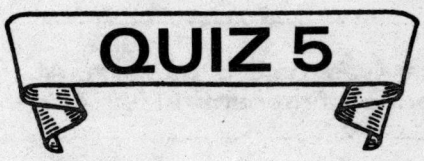

QUIZ 5

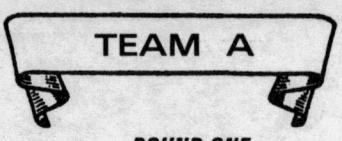

ROUND ONE
(Team Questions)

1 Q: What was the U.S. gangster Al
    Capone's first name in full?
   A: _ _ _ _ _ _ _ _ _ _ _ _ _ _ _ _   (p. 123)

●

2 Q: In which sport was the Dewar Cup
    competed for until 1976?
   A: _ _ _ _ _ _ _ _ _ _ _ _ _ _ _ _   (p. 123)

●

3 Q: What is the group name for wild geese
    in flight?
   A: _ _ _ _ _ _ _ _ _ _ _ _ _ _ _ _ _   (p. 123)

●

4 Q: Which famous American film star, born
    in 1913, was once and subsequently
    portrayed, a circus acrobat?
   A: _ _ _ _ _ _ _ _ _ _ _ _ _ _ _ _   (p. 123)

●

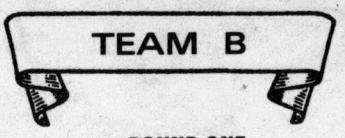

TEAM B

ROUND ONE
(Team Questions)

---

1 Q: What did the 'F' stand for in John F. Kennedy, the U.S. president from 1961—63?

A: _ _ _ _ _ _ _ _ _ _ _ _ _ _ _ (p. 125)

---●---

2 Q: Leander is the oldest amateur club in Britain, in which sport?

A: _ _ _ _ _ _ _ _ _ _ _ _ _ _ _ (p. 125)

---●---

3 Q: What is the group name for quail?

A: _ _ _ _ _ _ _ _ _ _ _ _ _ _ _ (p. 125)

---●---

4 Q: Which tough guy Welsh actor appeared and co-produced the 1963 film 'Zulu'?

A: _ _ _ _ _ _ _ _ _ _ _ _ _ _ _ (p. 125)

---●---

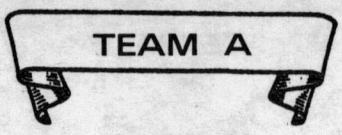

TEAM A

ROUND TWO
(Team Questions)

1 Q: Which member of the royal family
made his maiden speech in the House
of Lords in June 1984?

A: _ _ _ _ _ _ _ _ _ _ _ _ _ _ _ _ (p. 127)

2 Q: Which Evangelist preached a sermon at
Sandringham Parish Church in January
1984, at the invitation of H.M. the
Queen?

A: _ _ _ _ _ _ _ _ _ _ _ _ _ _ _ _ (p. 127)

3 Q: What was the name of the Soviet
Orbital Station in which three
cosmonauts set a space endurance
record in September 1984?

A: _ _ _ _ _ _ _ _ _ _ _ _ _ _ _ _ (p. 127)

4 Q: Which American soul singer was shot
dead by his father in April 1984?

A: _ _ _ _ _ _ _ _ _ _ _ _ _ _ _ _ (p. 127)

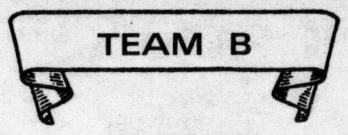

TEAM B

ROUND TWO
(Team Questions)

---

1 Q: In which hospital, in September 1984, was Prince Harry born?

A: _ _ _ _ _ _ _ _ _ _ _ _ _ _ _ (p. 129)

———————————●———————————

2 Q: Which Welsh operatic baritone made his last appearance at Covent Garden in June 1984?

A: _ _ _ _ _ _ _ _ _ _ _ _ _ _ _ _ (p. 129)

———————————●———————————

3 Q: A British Rail Advanced Passenger Train set a new speed record in December 1984, averaging 103 m.p.h. on a 232 minute journey from Euston to where?

A: _ _ _ _ _ _ _ _ _ _ _ _ _ _ _ (p. 129)

———————————●———————————

4 Q: Which popular singer was granted the Freedom of the city of Liverpool in November 1984?

A: _ _ _ _ _ _ _ _ _ _ _ _ _ _ _ (p. 129)

———————————●———————————

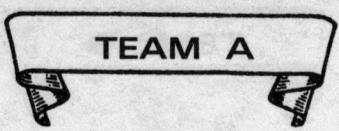

ROUND THREE
(Individual Questions: No conferring by either side)

1 Q: **What is known as Paddy's Lantern?**
 A: _ _ _ _ _ _ _ _ _ _ _ _ _ _ _ _ _ (p. 131)

⬤

2 Q: **A horse is measured in hands. What measurement is a hand in inches?**
 A: _ _ _ _ _ _ _ _ _ _ _ _ _ _ _ _ _ (p. 131)

⬤

3 Q: **What type of plant is a Kohlrabi (còal-ra-bee)?**
 A: _ _ _ _ _ _ _ _ _ _ _ _ _ _ _ _ _ (p. 131)

⬤

4 Q: **According to the saying, when, in Britain, should we 'not cast a clout'?**
 A: _ _ _ _ _ _ _ _ _ _ _ _ _ _ _ _ _ (p. 131)

⬤

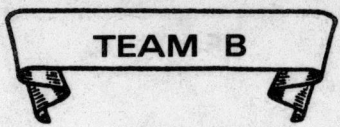

TEAM B

ROUND THREE
(Individual Questions: No conferring by either side)

1 Q: How does the U.S. military vehicle
'Jeep' derive it's name?
A: _ _ _ _ _ _ _ _ _ _ _ _ _ _ _ _ (p. 133)

●

2 Q: For how long was the fictional
character Rip Van Winkle supposed to
have slept before he woke to find the
world had completely changed?
A: _ _ _ _ _ _ _ _ _ _ _ _ _ _ _ _ (p. 133)

●

3 Q: What type of plant is a Ginkgo (jink-go)?
A: _ _ _ _ _ _ _ _ _ _ _ _ _ _ _ (p. 133)

●

4 Q: According to the saying, what, in
Britain, are we only supposed to eat
when there is a letter 'R' in the month?
A: _ _ _ _ _ _ _ _ _ _ _ _ _ _ _ (p. 134)

●

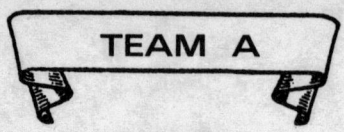

ROUND FOUR
(Team Questions)

1 Q: The Austral is which South American
   country's unit of currency?
   A: _ _ _ _ _ _ _ _ _ _ _ _ _ _ _ _ _ (p. 136)

2 Q: In which T.V. soap opera do the
   Ramsay family appear?
   A: _ _ _ _ _ _ _ _ _ _ _ _ _ _ _ _ (p. 137)

3 Q: Which silvery reactive metal
   discovered in 1808, by Sir Humphrey
   Davey, is used in X-rays?
   A: _ _ _ _ _ _ _ _ _ _ _ _ _ _ _ _ (p. 137)

4 Q: Which patron saint, who died in the 5th
   century A.D., has two emblems, one of
   which is a snake?
   A: _ _ _ _ _ _ _ _ _ _ _ _ _ _ _ _ (p. 137)

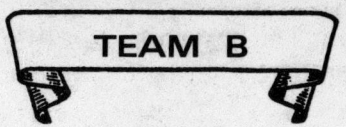

TEAM B

ROUND FOUR
(Team Questions)

---

1 Q: In which South American country do
one hundred Centavos = one Sucre?
A: _ _ _ _ _ _ _ _ _ _ _ _ _ _ _ _ _ (p. 139)

───────────●───────────

2 Q: The Tanner family appear in which
American T.V. series?
A: _ _ _ _ _ _ _ _ _ _ _ _ _ _ _ _ _ (p. 139)

───────────●───────────

3 Q: Which Radioactive Metallic Element,
first isolated in 1841, is used as a fuel
for Nuclear Reactors?
A: _ _ _ _ _ _ _ _ _ _ _ _ _ _ (pp. 139—40)

───────────●───────────

4 Q: The dove is the emblem of which
patron saint, who lived in the 6th
century A.D.?
A: _ _ _ _ _ _ _ _ _ _ _ _ _ _ _ _ _ (p. 140)

───────────●───────────

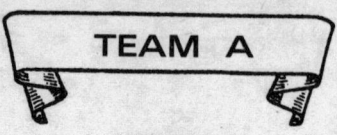

ROUND FIVE
(Team Questions)

---

1 Q: Name the leader of the Social
      Democrats in Portugal, who was
      re-elected as Prime Minister in the
      election in July 1987.

   A: _ _ _ _ _ _ _ _ _ _ _ _ _ _ _ _ (p. 142)

---

2 Q: Why was nineteen-year-old Matthias
      Rust from Hamburg facing court
      charges at the end of July 1987?

   A: _ _ _ _ _ _ _ _ _ _ _ _ _ _ _ _ (p. 142)

---

3 Q: Which sports personality was arrested
      after a domestic midnight shouting
      match in July 1987?

   A: _ _ _ _ _ _ _ _ _ _ _ _ _ _ _ _ (p. 143)

---

4 Q: U.K. Ministry of Agriculture officials
      were on the alert in July 1987 after
      something was discovered in food
      from a Bristol fruit market. What was
      it?

   A: _ _ _ _ _ _ _ _ _ _ _ _ _ _ _ _ (p. 143)

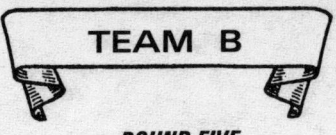

TEAM B

ROUND FIVE
(Team Questions)

---

1 Q: The youngest prime minister in the history of the republic of Italy was sworn in as leader of the new Italian government in July 1987. Name him.

A: _ _ _ _ _ _ _ _ _ _ _ _ _ _ _ _ (p. 145)

●

---

2 Q: Robert Anthony Cambridge of London was accused of committing criminal damage after a shotgun attack in July 1987. What suffered the damage?

A: _ _ _ _ _ _ _ _ _ _ _ _ _ _ _ _ (p. 145)

●

---

3 Q: Which sports personality was accused in July 1987, of placing bets on his own race?

A: _ _ _ _ _ _ _ _ _ _ _ _ _ _ _ _ (p. 145)

●

---

4 Q: Why were Aldrin, Dieldrin, and Endrin known collectively as the 'drins', a topic for discussion in the House of Lords in July 1987?

A: _ _ _ _ _ _ _ _ _ _ _ _ _ _ _ _ (p. 146)

●

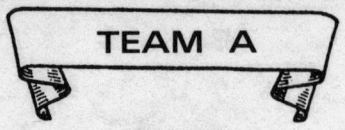

TEAM A

ROUND SIX
(Team Questions)

1 Q: Which member of the royal family is to
take part in 'Sporting Weekends with
the English Gentry', as sold to
American Tourists for 1987?
A: _ _ _ _ _ _ _ _ _ _ _ _ _ _ _ _ _ (p. 148)

●

2 Q: Who were the French brothers who
patented the cinematographe in 1895?
A: _ _ _ _ _ _ _ _ _ _ _ _ _ _ _ _ (p. 148)

●

3 Q: What was special about the shape of
the bomber aircraft the Avro Vulcan?
A: _ _ _ _ _ _ _ _ _ _ _ _ _ _ _ _ _ (p. 148)

●

4 Q: Which king was on the English throne
when Bonnie Prince Charlie was
defeated at the battle of Culloden?
A: _ _ _ _ _ _ _ _ _ _ _ _ _ _ _ _ (p. 148)

●

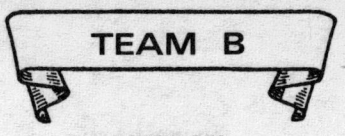

TEAM B

ROUND SIX
(Team Questions)

---

1 Q: Captain Phillips is to help manage a
three million pound Scottish equestrian
centre, in which famous sporting
locality?

A: _ _ _ _ _ _ _ _ _ _ _ _ _ _ _ _ (p. 150)

---•---

2 Q: Who were the French brothers who
made the first ascent in a hot-air
balloon?

A: _ _ _ _ _ _ _ _ _ _ _ _ _ _ _ _ (p. 150)

---•---

3 Q: What was the name given to the large
German rocket powered missile used in
World War II, especially to bombard
London?

A: _ _ _ _ _ _ _ _ _ _ _ _ _ _ _ _ (p. 150)

---•---

4 Q: At which battle was Henry VII
informally crowned in 1485?

A: _ _ _ _ _ _ _ _ _ _ _ _ _ _ _ (p. 150)

---•---

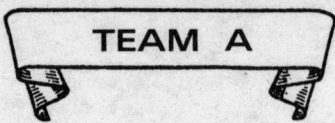

TEAM A

ROUND SEVEN
(Individual Questions: No conferring by either side)

1 Q: What is the name of the golf course
    near Southport Lancashire, that is on
    the rota for staging the Open
    championships?
  A: _ _ _ _ _ _ _ _ _ _ _ _ _ _ _ _ (p. 152)

2 Q: To qualify under normal circumstances
    for the Government's Cold Weather
    Payment, to what average level does
    the temperature have to fall?
  A: _ _ _ _ _ _ _ _ _ _ _ _ _ _ _ _ (p. 152)

3 Q: By what name is the tree Salix
    Babylonica better known (say-licks
    bab-ee-lon-icker)?
  A: _ _ _ _ _ _ _ _ _ _ _ _ _ _ _ _ (p. 152)

4 Q: Who was elected as MP for the
    parliamentary constituency of North
    Devon in 1974?
  A: _ _ _ _ _ _ _ _ _ _ _ _ _ _ _ _ (p. 152)

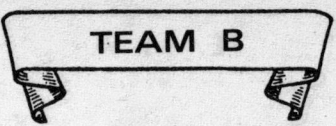

TEAM B

ROUND SEVEN
(Individual Questions: No conferring by either side)

---

1 Q: What is the name of the golf course
near Blackpool Lancashire, that is on
the rota for staging the Open
championships?

A: _ _ _ _ _ _ _ _ _ _ _ _ _ _ _ _   (p. 154)

---●---

2 Q: The seven day period of qualification
for the Government's Cold Weather
Payment, has to start on which day of
the week?

A: _ _ _ _ _ _ _ _ _ _ _ _ _ _ _   (p. 154)

---●---

3 Q: What are seeds of the Aesculus
Hippocastanum tree commonly known
as (ees-cue-lus   hippo-cass-tarnum)?

A: _ _ _ _ _ _ _ _ _ _ _ _ _ _ _ _   (p. 155)

---●---

4 Q: Who was elected as MP for the
parliamentary constituency Huyton in
Lancashire, in 1974?

A: _ _ _ _ _ _ _ _ _ _ _ _ _ _ _ _   (p. 155)

---●---

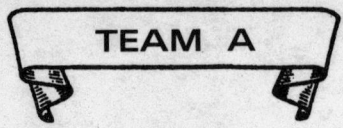

TEAM A

ROUND EIGHT
(Team Questions)

1 Q: What, in the Moslem world, are
      Minarets?
   A: _ _ _ _ _ _ _ _ _ _ _ _ _ _ _ _ (p. 157)

———————————— ● ————————————

2 Q: Which country was admitted to the
      Commonwealth in 1972, and the
      United Nations two years later?
   A: _ _ _ _ _ _ _ _ _ _ _ _ _ _ _ _ (p. 157)

———————————— ● ————————————

3 Q: Which medical word describes a
      deficiency of Haemoglobin, the
      Oxygen-carrying pigment in red cells?
   A: _ _ _ _ _ _ _ _ _ _ _ _ _ _ _ _ (p. 157)

———————————— ● ————————————

4 Q: Who was the male star of the 1978
      film 'Grease', about true love in the
      fifties?
   A: _ _ _ _ _ _ _ _ _ _ _ _ _ _ _ _ (p. 157)

———————————— ● ————————————

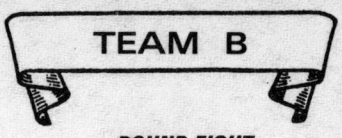

TEAM B

ROUND EIGHT
(Team Questions)

1 Q: What function is performed in the
     Muslim world, by the Mufti?
   A: _ _ _ _ _ _ _ _ _ _ _ _ _ _ _ _ (p. 159)

——————————●——————————

2 Q: Which country became a member of
     the Commonwealth in 1948, and a
     Republic in 1972?
   A: _ _ _ _ _ _ _ _ _ _ _ _ _ _ _ _ (p. 159)

——————————●——————————

3 Q: What name is given to the inherited
     disease in which one of the factors
     needed for blood clotting is missing?
   A: _ _ _ _ _ _ _ _ _ _ _ _ _ _ _ (p. 159)

——————————●——————————

4 Q: Which famous singer made his screen
     debut, in 1959 in the film 'Serious
     Charge'?
   A: _ _ _ _ _ _ _ _ _ _ _ _ _ _ _ (p. 159)

——————————●——————————

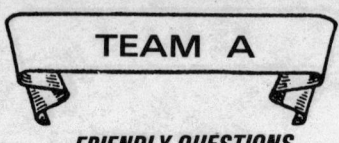

TEAM A

FRIENDLY QUESTIONS

1 Q: What was discovered at Rum Jungle, Northern Australia in 1952?

A: _ _ _ _ _ _ _ _ _ _ _ _ _ _ _ _ _ (p. 168)

●

2 Q: The Englishman Peter Collins was World Champion in 1976, in what sport?

A: _ _ _ _ _ _ _ _ _ _ _ _ _ _ _ _ _ (p. 168)

●

3 Q: What is a hunt which follows an artificial trail or scent instead of a live animal called?

A: _ _ _ _ _ _ _ _ _ _ _ _ _ _ _ _ _ (p. 168)

●

4 Q: What was rationalised as a result of the Jenkins report of 1962?

A: _ _ _ _ _ _ _ _ _ _ _ _ _ _ _ _ _ (p. 168)

●

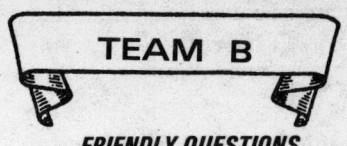

TEAM B

FRIENDLY QUESTIONS

---

1 Q: What is the highest waterfall in the world?

A: _ _ _ _ _ _ _ _ _ _ _ _ _ _ _ _ (p. 169)

——————————— ● ———————————

2 Q: The 'Cincinnati Reds' team were World Champions in 1975 and 76, in what sport?

A: _ _ _ _ _ _ _ _ _ _ _ _ _ _ _ _ (p. 169)

——————————— ● ———————————

3 Q: What are 'snaffles' and 'pelhams'?

A: _ _ _ _ _ _ _ _ _ _ _ _ _ _ _ (p. 169)

——————————— ● ———————————

4 Q: What is the French equivalent of the Stock Exchange called?

A: _ _ _ _ _ _ _ _ _ _ _ _ _ _ _ _ (p. 169)

——————————— ● ———————————

INTERESTING FACT:
A secret tunnel once led from the local church to the Bowling Green pub in Wrexham. It is thought that this was for the convenience of the monks.

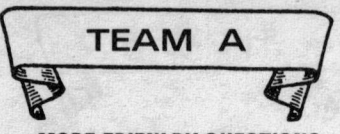

TEAM A

MORE FRIENLDY QUESTIONS

---

1 Q: In the international C.G.S. measurement system, what does the initial 'S' represent?

A: _ _ _ _ _ _ _ _ _ _ _ _ _ _ _ _ _ (p. 168)

---

2 Q: Who was the American baseball star at one time married to Marilyn Monroe?

A: _ _ _ _ _ _ _ _ _ _ _ _ _ _ _ _ (p. 168)

---

3 Q: Which nation built the ocean liner 'Normandie' in 1931?

A: _ _ _ _ _ _ _ _ _ _ _ _ _ _ _ _ (p. 168)

---

4 Q: What is the opposite of Centrifugal, as in centrifugal force?

A: _ _ _ _ _ _ _ _ _ _ _ _ _ _ _ _ (p. 168)

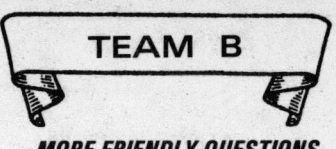

TEAM B

MORE FRIENDLY QUESTIONS

1 Q: In physics, what is the heat required to raise one gramme of water one degree centigrade called?

A: _ _ _ _ _ _ _ _ _ _ _ _ _ _ _ _ (p. 169)

●

2 Q: Who is the American film star married to the tennis player John McEnroe?

A: _ _ _ _ _ _ _ _ _ _ _ _ _ _ _ _ (p. 169)

●

3 Q: Which nation re-built the famous transatlantic ocean liner the 'Bremen' in 1955?

A: _ _ _ _ _ _ _ _ _ _ _ _ _ _ _ _ (p. 169)

●

4 Q: What is the opposite of fission, as in nuclear fission?

A: _ _ _ _ _ _ _ _ _ _ _ _ _ _ _ _ (p. 169)

●

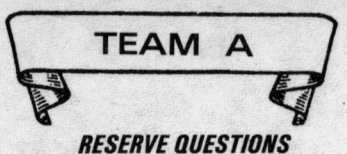

TEAM A

RESERVE QUESTIONS

1 Q: Who originally played the part of
Brother Dominic in the British TV series
'Oh Brother' in 1970?
A: _ _ _ _ _ _ _ _ _ _ _ _ _ _ _ _ (p. 168)

●

2 Q: Of what American state is Baton Rouge
the capital?
A: _ _ _ _ _ _ _ _ _ _ _ _ _ _ _ _ (p. 168)

●

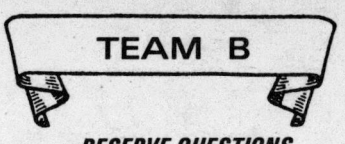

TEAM B

RESERVE QUESTIONS

1 Q: Name the animated dog who starred in
the children's TV programme 'Magic
Roundabout' in the 1960s.
   A: _ _ _ _ _ _ _ _ _ _ _ _ _ _ _ _ _ (p. 169)

2 Q: Of what American state is Charleston
the capital?
   A: _ _ _ _ _ _ _ _ _ _ _ _ _ _ _ _ _ (p. 169)

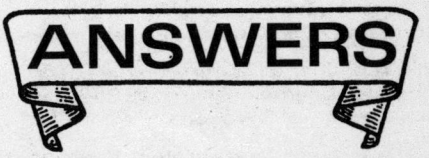

QUIZ 1
ROUND ONE
(Team Questions)

1 Q: What is the name of the largest soccer stadium in Glasgow, Scotland?
   A: **Hampden Park.**

2 Q: In terms of angle measurement how many degrees are there in a turn and a half?
   A: **540 degrees (360 degrees in each complete turn).**

3 Q: Which continental golfer won the Epson (not Epsom) Matchplay Championship in 1987?
   A: **Mats Lanner, of Sweden.**

4 Q: What substance found in every home has the chemical formula $C_{12}H_{22}O_{11}$?
   A: **Sugar (called sucrose or saccharose).**

QUIZ 2
ROUND ONE
(Team Questions)

1 Q: Which mountain chain is deemed as forming the Eastern boundary to Europe?
   A: **The Urals (in the Soviet Union, over 2,000 km from the Arctic Ocean to the Aral Sea).**

2 Q: What was the nationality of Sonja Henie, the figureskater, who died in 1969?
   A: **Norwegian.**

3 Q: Who was the first English soccer player to have won over one hundred international caps?
   A: **Billy Wright.**

4 Q: What would you be suffering if you were treated with 'ignominy'?
   A: **Public disgrace or shame, dishonour.**

QUIZ 3
ROUND ONE
(Team Questions)

1 Q: By what name do we know the North African country who's Arabic name, Al-Maghreb means farthest west?
   A: **Morocco.**

2 Q: What name is given to the ornamental plate around a key hole, which protects the surface of the door?

A: An escutcheon (air-scut-shun-plate).

3 Q: Who starred opposite Yul Brynner in the 1956 musical film 'The King and I'?
A: Deborah Kerr.

4 Q: How many numbered slots are there on a standard roulette wheel, used in gambling?
A: Thirty-seven (accept thirty-eight).

QUIZ 4
ROUND ONE
(Team Questions)

1 Q: When crossing the International Date Line, what happens to the date when travelling from West to East?
A: The date is put back a day.

2 Q: In which country was former U.S. Secretary of State, Henry Kissinger born?
A: Germany (born 1923).

3 Q: What is a 'turbo-prop' aeroplane?
A: An aeroplane whose engine uses a (gas) turbine to drive a propellor.

4 Q: What Essex-born author wrote the novel 'The French Lieutenant's Woman' and a philosophical study called 'The Aristos'?
A: John Fowles.

QUIZ 5
ROUND ONE
(Team Questions)

1 Q: What was the U.S. gangster Al Capone's first name in full?
A: Alphonse.

2 Q: In which sport was the Dewar Cup competed for until 1976?
A: Tennis (British Indoor tournaments from 1968—76).

3 Q: What is the group name for wild geese in flight?
A: Skein.

4 Q: Which famous American film star, born in 1913, was once, and subsequently portrayed, a circus acrobat?
A: Burt Lancaster.

QUIZ 1
ROUND ONE
(Team Questions)

1 Q: The Traitor's Gate is part of which famous building in Britain?
   A: **Tower of London (the old water gate to the Thames where many state prisoners were brought).**

2 Q: The S.I. unit of a joule is a measurement of what, specifically?
   A: **Energy or work (when a force of one Newton is displaced through one metre in that direction).**

3 Q: In 1985 the United States lost the Ryder Cup golf tournament for the first time since. . . . when?
   A: **1957 (allow two years either way) when Great Britain won at Lindrick, Yorkshire.**

4 Q: Which chemical element is represented by the letter 'F'?
   A: **Fluorine (toxic, pale yellow halogen gas).**

QUIZ 2
ROUND ONE
(Team Questions)

1 Q: In which ocean are the Maldive, Chagos and Cocos Islands situated?
   A: **The Indian Ocean.**

2 Q: What was the nationality of the World Heavyweight Boxing champion, Primo Carnera?
   A: **Italian.**

3 Q: Who was the first soccer Footballer of the Year in 1946/7?
   A: **Sir Stanley Matthews.**

4 Q: What does it mean to do something with 'celerity'?
   A: **Quickness, rapidity of motion, i.e. anything that was done quickly.**

QUIZ 3
ROUND ONE
(Team Questions)

1 Q: What North African republic is situated between Algeria to the west and Libya to the south east?
   A: **Tunisia.**

2 Q: In art, what name is given to a pair of pictures
       (artworks) hinged together?
   A: **A diptych (dip-tick).**

3 Q: Kirk Douglas played the wild west outlaw Doc
       Holliday in the 1957 western film 'Gunfight at the
       O.K. Corral'. Who played Wyatt Earp?
   A: **Burt Lancaster.**

4 Q: On a standard roulette wheel used in gambling, what
       colour is the zero slot?
   A: **Green.**

QUIZ 4
ROUND ONE
(Team Questions)

1 Q: Which European explorer discovered Lake Victoria
       which was believed to be the source of the River
       Nile?
   A: **John Speke (British explorer in 1858).**

2 Q: In which country was the mountaineer and explorer
       Sir Edmund Hillary, who climbed Mount Everest,
       born?
   A: **New Zealand (in 1919).**

3 Q: What was a 'flying-boat'?
   A: **An aircraft with a fuselage that floats on water.**

4 Q: Name the American who was a leading man in many
       1940s films, and published his autobiography in
       1965 called 'Where's the Rest of Me'?
   A: **Ronald Reagan.**

QUIZ 5
ROUND ONE
(Team Questions)

1 Q: What did the 'F' stand for in John F. Kennedy, the
       U.S. president from 1961–63?
   A: **Fitzgerald.**

2 Q: Leander is the oldest amateur club in Britain, in which
       sport?
   A: **Rowing (originated in 1818 in London; now at
       Henley-on-Thames).**

3 Q: What is the group name for quail?
   A: **Bevy, covey or jug.**

4 Q: Which tough guy Welsh actor appeared and
       co-produced the 1963 film 'Zulu'?
   A: **(Sir) Stanley Baker (died 1976).**

QUIZ 1
ROUND TWO
(Team Questions)

1 Q: Which former British Prime Minister was appointed a Knight of the Garter in April 1976?
   A: **Harold Wilson (Lord Wilson of Rievaulx).**

2 Q: The owner of 'The Times' newspaper died in August 1976. What was his name?
   A: **Lord Thomson of Fleet.**

3 Q: On which island, in March 1977, did two Jumbo Jets collide in what was claimed to be the world's worst aircraft disaster?
   A: **Tenerife (581 killed).**

4 Q: Which British driver won the Grand Prix World Drivers' Championship in 1976?
   A: **James Hunt (driving a MacLaren).**

QUIZ 2
ROUND TWO
(Team Questions)

1 Q: 'It's Over' was a number one hit, in Britain, in 1964, for which popular singer?
   A: **Roy Orbison (known as Big O).**

2 Q: Which tunnel between Switzerland and Italy, was completed in March 1964?
   A: **Great St. Bernard Tunnel.**

3 Q: When Harold Wilson formed a Labour government in 1964, who was his first Home Secretary?
   A: **Sir Frank Soskice.**

4 Q: Which British athlete won the women's long jump at the 1964 Olympic Games?
   A: **Mary Rand (6.76 metres).**

QUIZ 3
ROUND TWO
(Team Questions)

1 Q: Who was granted the title of Prince of the United Kingdom in 1957?
   A: **Duke of Edinburgh.**

2 Q: This famous Italian conductor began his career as a cellist, and died in 1957. Who was he?
   A: **Arturo Toscanini (1867–1957).**

3 Q: Near which island in the central Pacific, did Britain explode her first H-bomb in 1957?
   A: **Christmas Island.**

4 Q: Who resigned as Britain's Prime Minister in January 1957?
   A: **Sir Anthony Eden.**

QUIZ 4
ROUND TWO
(Team Questions)

1 Q: In August 1965 what product was banned from advertising in TV commercials in Britain?
   A: **Cigarettes.**

2 Q: Name the Egyptian ex-king died in March 1965 aged forty five.
   A: **Ex-King Farouk of Egypt. (reigned 1937–52).**

3 Q: In, 1965, Karen Muir set up a women's sporting record aged only twelve years. Which sport?
   A: **Swimming. (110 yards backstroke).**

4 Q: In May 1965 Franz Jonas was elected president of which country in Europe?
   A: **Austria.**

QUIZ 5
ROUND TWO
(Team Questions)

1 Q: Which member of the royal family made his maiden speech in the House of Lords in June 1984?
   A: **H.R.H. the Duke of Gloucester.**

2 Q: Which Evangelist preached a sermon at Sandringham Parish Church in January 1984, at the invitation of H.M. the Queen?
   A: **Dr Billy Graham.**

3 Q: What was the name of the Soviet Orbital Station in which three cosmonauts set a space endurance record in September 1984?
   A: **Salyut 7 (212 days).**

4 Q: Which American soul singer was shot dead by his father in April 1984?
   A: **Marvin Gaye (on the eve of his 45th birthday).**

QUIZ 1
ROUND TWO
(Team Questions)

1 Q: Who became Britain's Prime Minister in April 1976?
   A: **James Callaghan.**

2 Q: In November 1976, the American oilgroup Atlantic Richfield took control of which National British newspaper?
   A: **The 'Observer'. (sold to Roland Rowland in 1981).**

3 Q: Which country was affected, in July 1976, by the world's worst earthquake (in terms of number killed) for over four hundred years?
   A: **China (8.2 Richter Scale — 800,000+ killed).**

4 Q: Who, in 1976, became the first British male since 1908 to win an Olympic swimming Gold Medal?
   A: **David Wilkie (two hundred metres breaststroke in world record time).**

QUIZ 2
ROUND TWO
(Team Questions)

1 Q: The Kinks topped the British charts in 1964. Name the song they took to No. 1?
   A: **'You Really Got Me'.**

2 Q: The Verrazano-Narrows Suspension Bridge was opened in November 1964. In which city is it?
   A: **New York.**

3 Q: Harold Wilson became British Prime Minister in 1964. Who was his first Foreign Secretary?
   A: **Patrick Gordon Walker.**

4 Q: Which British athlete won the men's long jump at the 1964 Olympic Games?
   A: **Lynn Davies (8.07 metres).**

QUIZ 3
ROUND TWO
(Team Questions)

1 Q: What was significant about H.M. the Queen's 1957 Christmas broadcast?
   A: **It was televised for the first time.**

2 Q: The composer of the symphonic poems 'Kullervo' and 'Finlandia' died in 1957. Who was he?
   A: **Jean Sibelius (1865–1957).**

3 Q: One of the world's largest radio telescope was put
    into operation for Manchester University in 1957.
    Where was it situated?
  A: **Jodrell Bank (in Cheshire).**

4 Q: Who was appointed Britain's Prime Minister in
    January 1957?
  A: **Harold MacMillan.**

QUIZ 4
ROUND TWO
(Team Questions)

1 Q: Name the most popular offshore pirate commercial
    radio station which was established in 1965 close to
    Britain.
  A: **Radio Caroline.**

2 Q: Name the musical "King" who died in February
    1965, at the age of forty five.
  A: **Nat "King" Cole. (American black pianist and
    singer).**

3 Q: In July 1965, Madame Vaucher became the first
    woman to achieve what sporting accomplishment?
  A: **Climbing the Matterhorn. (North Wall).**

4 Q: Name the Black Muslim leader who was shot dead in
    Manhattan, USA, in February 1965.
  A: **Malcolm X.**

QUIZ 5
ROUND TWO
(Team Questions)

1 Q: In which hospital, in September 1984, was Prince
    Harry born?
  A: **St. Mary's Hospital (in London).**

2 Q: Which Welsh operatic baritone made his last
    appearance at Covent Garden in June 1984?
  A: **Sir Geraint Evans.**

3 Q: A British Rail Advanced Passenger Train set a new
    speed record in December 1984, averaging 103
    m.p.h on a 232 minute journey from Euston to
    where?
  A: **Glasgow (401 miles).**

4 Q: Which popular singer was granted the Freedom of
    the city of Liverpool in November 1984?
  A: **Paul McCartney.**

QUIZ 1
ROUND THREE
(Individual Questions: No conferring by either side)

1 Q: What computer programming language is named
       after a 17th century French mathematician who, at
       the age of 19, invented the first adding machine?
   A: **Pascal (after Blaise Pascal, author of the
       'Pensees'.**

2 Q: Which English peninsula is formed by the estuaries of
       the Mersey and the Dee?
   A: **Wirral.**

3 Q: What are Ishihara charts used to determine?
   A: **Colour blindness (the charts, designed by the
       Japanese specialist, Shinobu Ishihara).**

4 Q: On a coat of arms what did a 'bend sinister' signify?
   A: **Illegitimacy. (a diagonal line disecting from top
       right to bottom left indicating a bastard line).**

QUIZ 2
ROUND THREE
(Individual Questions: No conferring by either side)

1 Q: The U.S. composer Jerome Kern, wrote the music
       for which stage musical, first performed in 1927?
   A: **'Showboat'.**

2 Q: Which famous person did Sirhan Sirhan assassinate?
   A: **Senator Robert F. Kennedy (in 1968).**

3 Q: Who directed the films 'The Godfather' in 1972 and
       'Apocalypse Now' in 1979?
   A: **Francis Ford Coppola (American director).**

4 Q: In what year did the British Labour party first form a
       government?
   A: **1924 (led by Ramsay MacDonald).**

QUIZ 3
ROUND THREE
(Individual Questions: No conferring by either side)

1 Q: In physics what name is given to the study of gases
       in motion?
   A: **Aerodynamics.**

2 Q: What are 'petit pois' (petty pwar) found on a french
       menu?
   A: **Small peas (small sweet french green peas).**

3 Q: Which English girl won both the one hundred metres and two hundred metres in the 1962 Commonwealth Games?
A: **Dorothy Hyman, with 11.2 seconds and 23.8 seconds.**

4 Q: Why was the former Cabinet Minister James Prior so upset in December 1986 when the government decided not to buy the GEC Nimrod airborne warning system?
A: **He is Chairman of GEC.**

QUIZ 4
ROUND THREE
(Individual Questions: No conferring by either side)

1 Q: Give the name of Sweden's parliament
A: **The Riksdag.**

2 Q: Which American novelist wrote *A Portrait of a Lady?*
A: **Henry James.**

3 Q: Under which sign of the Zodiac is a birthday on 5th November?
A: **Scorpio (Oct. 23rd—Nov. 21st; the Scorpion).**

4 Q: Name the Emperor of Japan during the second World War.
A: **Hirohito (from 1926; became a constitutional monarch in 1946).**

QUIZ 5
ROUND THREE
(Individual Questions: No conferring by either side)

1 Q: What is known as Paddy's Lantern?
A: **The Moon (used by sailors — after Parish-lantern).**

2 Q: A horse is measured in hands. What measurement is a hand in inches?
A: **Four inches.**

3 Q: What type of plant is a Kohlrabi (coal-ra-bee)?
A: **A vegetable, type of cabbage of which the stem is eaten.**

4 Q: According to the saying, when, in Britain, should we 'not cast a clout'?
A: **'Before May is out'.**

QUIZ 1
ROUND THREE
(Individual Questions: No conferring by either side)

1 Q: Who worked for nearly forty years on the uncompleted 'Difference Engine', a 19th century fore-runner of the analytic computer?
  A: **Charles Babbage.**

2 Q: What is the area of water flanked by Gibraltar Point and Hunstanton Point known as?
  A: **The Wash.**

3 Q: Who was the English physicist, a sufferer himself, who first described colour blindness?
  A: **John Dalton (hence it is also sometimes called Daltonism).**

4 Q: In heraldry, what does the term 'dexter' mean?
  A: **Refer the right side of a Shield of Arms (opposite to sinister — on the spectator's left).**

QUIZ 2
ROUND THREE
(Individual Questions: No conferring by either side)

1 Q: Lionel Bart wrote the words and music for which stage musical, first performed in London in 1960?
  A: **'Oliver' (adaptation of Charles Dickens' 'Oliver Twist').**

2 Q: Which famous person was assassinated by James Earl Ray?
  A: **Martin Luther King (in 1968; U.S. civil rights leader).**

3 Q: Who directed the films 'Jaws' in 1975 and 'Close Encounters of the Third Kind' in 1977?
  A: **Steven Spielberg (American director).**

4 Q: In what year was the naval Battle of the River Plate?
  A: **1939 (Second World War; between the Graf Spee German battleship and British Cruisers).**

QUIZ 3
ROUND THREE
(Individual Questions: No conferring by either side)

1 Q: In chemistry what name is given to the suspension of a liquid in a gas?
  A: **An aerosol.**

2 Q: What does the french word 'coq' (cock) refer to on a menu?
A: **Chicken (as in 'coq au vin'; in wine).**

3 Q: Who won the shot putt for Britain in the Commonwealth Games of 1974 and 1978?
A: **Geoff Capes, now sometimes known as the world's strongest man.**

4 Q: What type of aircraft will the RAF continue to use for airborne radar cover until the arrival of the AWACS system in 1991?
A: **Shackletons (now forty years old).**

QUIZ 4
ROUND THREE
(Individual Questions: No conferring by either side)

1 Q: In which country is the port of Europoort?
A: **Holland/Netherlands (near Rotterdam).**

2 Q: Which novelist and playwright wrote *The Picture of Dorian Grey?*
A: **Oscar Wilde.**

3 Q: Under which sign of the Zodiac is a birthday on 25th December?
A: **Capricorn (the Goat, December 22nd—January 19th).**

4 Q: In 1944 paratroops were dropped on a Dutch town as part of an Allied plan to shorten the second World War, but the plan ended in disaster. Name the town.
A: **Arnhem (in E. Netherlands on the Rhine).**

QUIZ 5
ROUND THREE
(Individual Questions: No conferring by either side)

1 Q: How does the U.S. military vehicle 'Jeep' derive it's name?
A: **From GP, General Purpose Vehicle.**

2 Q: For how long was the fictional character Rip Van Winkle supposed to have slept before he woke to find the world had completely changed?
A: **Twenty years (story by W. Irving 1820).**

3 Q: What type of plant is a Ginkgo (jink-go)?
A: **A tree (Chinese ornamental tree, also called maidenhair tree).**

4 Q: According to the saying, what, in Britain, are we only
        supposed to eat when there is a letter 'R' in the
        month?
   A: **Oysters (i.e. from September to April which is the
        normal marketing time).**

QUIZ 1
ROUND FOUR
(Team Questions)

1 Q: Which British Prime Minister was famous for changing into evening dress before writing his novels?

  A: **Benjamin Disraeli (1804—81 novels include 'Sybil' and 'Coningsby').**

2 Q: What is the most common family surname in the world, of which there are over 104 million people with the name?

  A: **Chang (Chinese name; approx. eleven per cent of their population).**

3 Q: Which single word in the English language has the most meanings, having 58 noun, 126 verbal and 10 partial adjective uses?

  A: **Set.**

4 Q: Which fruit bears the largest known seed in the world, which may weigh up to 40 lb?

  A: **Double coconut or Coco de Mer (of the Seychelles).**

QUIZ 2
ROUND FOUR
(Team Questions)

1 Q: The rhyme entitled 'The Jackdaw of Rheims' is from which collection of poems and stories?

  A: **The 'Ingoldsby Legends' (by R.H. Barham in 1837).**

2 Q: Complete the following proverb 'Two's company. . . . .'?

  A: **. . . Three's a crowd (or 'is none'; often used by lovers).**

3 Q: In terms of transport what does the term cloverleaf apply to?

  A: **Road junction (resembling four-leaf clover in form) that joins two intersecting main roads.**

4 Q: Which British pop group's first number one single in the U.K. was called 'Down Down'?

  A: **Status Quo.**

QUIZ 3
ROUND FOUR
(Team Questions)

1 Q: Who was the composer of the 'Bear Symphony' in 1786?
  A: Haydn (Joseph; Austrian composer. Symphony No. 82 in C).

2 Q: What are culottes?
  A: Womens wide flared trousers designed to resemble a skirt, a divided skirt.

3 Q: In which novel does the middle-aged Jewish musician 'Svengali' appear?
  A: 'Trilby' (by George du Maurier 1894).

4 Q: In which film did Tony Curtis and Jack Lemon both disguise themselves as girl musicians?
  A: 'Some Like it Hot' (1959, also starring Marilyn Monroe).

QUIZ 4
ROUND FOUR
(Team Questions)

1 Q: Which former Duke of Bohemia is well known to us through Christmas Carols?
  A: King Wenceslas or Wenceslaus (10th century; patron saint of Czechoslovakia).

2 Q: Who was the Biblical Old Testament David, King of the Hebrew's son?
  A: Solomon (King of Israel 10 B.C.; credited with great wisdom).

3 Q: Which American actor said of himself, 'I have eyes like those of a dead pig'?
  A: Marlon Brando (films include 'The Godfather' 1972 and 'On the Waterfront' 1954).

4 Q: Who was the youngest soccer player to first score 100 goals in the English football league?
  A: Jimmy Greaves (Chelsea; 20 years 9 months).

QUIZ 5
ROUND FOUR
(Team Questions)

1 Q: The Austral is which South American country's unit of currency?
  A: Argentina (1000 Pesos = = 1 Austral).

2 Q: In which T.V. soap opera do the Ramsay family appear?
   A: **'Neighbours'.**

3 Q: Which silvery reactive metal discovered in 1808, by Sir Humphrey Davey, is used in X-rays?
   A: **Barium (Barium Carbonate is used as rat poison).**

4 Q: Which patron saint, who died in the 5th century A.D., has two emblems, one of which is a snake?
   A: **St. Patrick (the shamrock is the other).**

QUIZ 1
ROUND FOUR
(Team Questions)

1 Q: Which famous 19th century classical author could only write when facing north?
   A: **Charles Dickens (1812—70; novels include 'Bleak House').**

2 Q: What is the Indian family surname which means 'In Secret', of which there were 90,000 people with the name in Britain in 1984?
   A: **Singh.**

3 Q: Which single word in the English language has the most homophones (various spellings and meanings but pronounced the same)?
   A: **Air (38 in all).**

4 Q: Which tree bears the largest known leaves of any plant in the world, which may measure up to 65 ft. in length of the blade?
   A: **Raffia Palm or Bamboo Palm.**

QUIZ 2
ROUND FOUR
(Team Questions)

1 Q: Who wrote the adventure novel 'The Last of the Mohicans'?
   A: **James Fenimore Cooper (U.S. author with naval background; written in 1826).**

2 Q: Complete the following saying 'Dead men tell. . . . .?
   A: **. . . No tales (or lies; meaning a person cannot talk if he is dead).**

3 Q: In terms of transport what is a 'permanent way' in Britain?
   A: **A railway track.**

4 Q: Which British Pop group's first number one single in the U.K. was called 'Hot Love'?
   A: **T. Rex.**

QUIZ 3
ROUND FOUR
(Team Questions)

1 Q: Which composer told in music the story of an
afternoon in the life of a fawn in 1894?
  A: **Debussy (Claude, French composer).**

2 Q: From what source does Castor Oil come?
  A: **The Castor Bean or Castor Oil plant.**

3 Q: In Greek legend Penelope was the wife of whom?
  A: **Ulysses (or Odysseus. She was portrayed as a
model of all domestic virtues in Homer's 'Iliad').**

4 Q: Who starred as country singer Loretta Lynn in the
1980 film 'Coal Miner's Daughter'?
  A: **Sissy Spacek.**

QUIZ 4
ROUND FOUR
(Team Questions)

1 Q: What was the name of the girl featured in the stories
of Robin Hood?
  A: **Maid Marian.**

2 Q: What name is given to the monk in charge of an
abbey in the Catholic church?
  A: **Abbot.**

3 Q: Who painted a famous self-portrait in 1745 entitled
'Self Portrait with Dog'?
  A: **William Hogarth (English engraver and painter
1697–1764).**

4 Q: Who was Fulham's most capped International soccer
player; from 1954–62?
  A: **Johnny Haynes.**

QUIZ 5
ROUND FOUR
(Team Questions)

1 Q: In which South American country do one hundred
Centavos = one Sucre?
  A: **Ecuador.**

2 Q: The Tanner family appear in which American T.V.
series?
  A: **A.L.F. (alien life form).**

3 Q: Which Radioactive Metallic Element, first isolated in
1841, is used as a fuel for Nuclear Reactors?

A: Uranium (first isolated by E. Peligot).

4 Q: The dove is the emblem of which patron saint, who lived in the 6th century A.D.?

A: St. David (patron saint of Wales).

QUIZ 1
ROUND FIVE
(Team Questions)

1 Q: In horse-racing what is a male, ungelded horse up to four years old called?
   A: **Colt.**

2 Q: Who expanded her music business career into Hollywood in 1972 with her starring role in 'Lady Sings the Blues'?
   A: **Diana Ross (followed by 'Mahogany' in 1975).**

3 Q: Which city is joined to Moscow by the trans-Siberian railway?
   A: **Vladivostok.**

4 Q: In which country, in August 1987, was Prime Minister David Lange returned to power for a second three-year term?
   A: **New Zealand.**

QUIZ 2
ROUND FIVE
(Team Questions)

1 Q: Which country's naval manoeuvres in the summer of 1987, were codenamed 'Operation Martyrdom'?
   A: **Iran (in the Strait of Hormuz).**

2 Q: What caused a British Army vet to be flown out to Gibraltar in August 1987?
   A: **A chest virus threatening the Rock's Colony of Barbary Apes.**

3 Q: A Leonardo Da Vinci cartoon was in the news in July 1987. Why?
   A: **It was damaged in the National Gallery (by Robert Cambridge).**

4 Q: The 1987 film 'Who's That Girl' was slammed by U.S. critics. Who is the star of the film?
   A: **Madonna.**

QUIZ 3
ROUND FIVE
(Team Questions)

1 Q: What do Americans Jim and Tammy Bakker and Jerry Falwell have in common?
   A: **They are all Evangelists.**

2 Q: Which former Labour MP, in August 1987, denied
      allegations that he had been a Czech. spy?
   A: **John Stonehouse (alleged in Peter Wright's book
      'Spycatcher').**

3 Q: What was unusual about the return of Poppy, a lost
      budgerigar, to her Bristol owner in August 1987?
   A: **Poppy told the couple who found her, her name
      and address.**

4 Q: The 10th anniversary of whose death was
      celebrated with documentaries and films on T.V
      during the summer of 1987?
   A: **Elvis Presley.**

QUIZ 4
ROUND FIVE
(Team Questions)

1 Q: Actress Michelle Dotrice is married to the star of the
      T.V. series 'The Equalizer'. Who is he?
   A: **Edward Woodward.**

2 Q: Which journey, first taken in 1787, did the square-
      rigged sailing ship 'Young Endeavour' begin in July
      1987?
   A: **England to Australia.**

3 Q: At which research centre did British servicemen
      allege, in July 1987, that they had suffered injuries in
      lethal nerve gas tests?
   A: **Porton Down.**

4 Q: Which American sportswear firm did the remaining
      Beatles decide to sue, in July 1987, for unauthorised
      use of one of their recordings in an advert?
   A: **Nike (the song was 'Revolution').**

QUIZ 5
ROUND FIVE
(Team Questions)

1 Q: Name the leader of the Social Democrats in Portugal,
      who was re-elected as Prime Minister in the election
      in July 1987.
   A: **Anibal Cavaco Silva.**

2 Q: Why was nineteen-year-old Matthias Rust from
      Hamburg facing court charges at the end of July
      1987?
   A: **Landing his plane in Red Square, Moscow,
      violating international flight rules.**

3 Q: Which sports personality was arrested after a
       domestic midnight shouting match in July 1987?
   A: **Alex 'Hurricane' Higgins (former world snooker
       champion).**

4 Q: U.K. Ministry of Agriculture officials were on the alert
       in July 1987 after something was discovered in food
       from a Bristol fruit market. What was it?
   A: **A colorado beetle (found in a box of peaches).**

QUIZ 1
ROUND FIVE
(Team Questions)

1 Q: In horse-racing, what is a female horse up to four years old called?
   A: **Filly.**

2 Q: Which British rock star pursued his developing acting career in the 1978 film, 'Just a Gigolo'?
   A: **David Bowie.**

3 Q: Which city is the Southern Terminal for the 'Orient Express'?
   A: **Istanbul.**

4 Q: The Nazi Rudolf Hess died in August 1987, aged 93. In which prison was he held for 41 years?
   A: **Spandau (in Berlin).**

QUIZ 2
ROUND FIVE
(Team Questions)

1 Q: What nationality was Military Attaché Ivan Djambov ordered out of Britain in July 1987?
   A: **Bulgarian.**

2 Q: Which English actress is the leading figure in the Animal Welfare Group 'Zoo Check'?
   A: **Virginnia McKenna (starred as Joy Adamson in the film 'Born Free').**

3 Q: Which fast-food chain announced in August 1987, that after ten years of negotiations, it would be opening three branches in Russia?
   A: **MacDonalds.**

4 Q: Who is the author of the 1987 book 'Cricket XXXX Cricket'?
   A: **Frances Edmonds (wife of England cricketer Phil Edmonds).**

QUIZ 3
ROUND FIVE
(Team Questions)

1 Q: Which comedian was banned from driving for three years in August 1987, after inviting a policeman to 'nick' him after he had been drinking?
   A: **Jim Davidson (catchphrase 'nick nick').**

2 Q: A chairman of the Lonrho business group, he is a former Chairman of the Conservative party. Name him.
A: **Edward Du Cann.**

3 Q: American Jim Dickson began an attempted crossing of the Atlantic in August 1987. What made his attempt unusual?
A: **He is blind (the first blind person to attempt it).**

4 Q: Complete the title of the 1987 feature length cartoon 'Pinocchio and the. . . . .?
A: **. . . . .Emperor of the Night.'**

QUIZ 4
ROUND FIVE
(Team Questions)

1 Q: In which T.V. series shown on Channel 4, did Ed Asner star as the editor of the 'Los Angeles Tribune'?
A: **Lou Grant.**

2 Q: What did Concorde smash in a record breaking time of 103 minutes in July 1987?
A: **The Transatlantic Speed Record.**

3 Q: Why were Soviet workers Viktor Bryukhanov, Nikolai Fomin and Anatoly Dyatlov all gaoled in July 1987?
A: **Because they were held responsible for the Chernobyl disaster.**

4 Q: Which product was advertised, for the first time ever on Britain's T.V. screens, on 1st August, 1987?
A: **Condoms.**

QUIZ 5
ROUND FIVE
(Team Questions)

1 Q: The youngest prime minister in the history of the republic of Italy was sworn in as leader of the new Italian government in July 1987. Name him.
A: **Giovanni Goria (aged 43, Christian Democrat).**

2 Q: Robert Anthony Cambridge of London was accused of committing criminal damage after a shotgun attack in July 1987. What suffered the damage?
A: **A Leonardo da Vinci cartoon in the National Gallery, London.**

3 Q: Which sports personality was accused in July 1987, of placing bets on his own race?
A: **Lester Piggott (ex-champion horse racing jockey).**

4 Q: Why were Aldrin, Dieldrin, and Endrin known
    collectively as the 'drins', a topic for discussion in the
    House of Lords in July 1987?
  A: **Pesticides which are highly toxic; calling for a ban
    on the use of them.**

QUIZ 1
ROUND SIX
(Team Questions)

1 Q: What name is given to the rules which govern the work of the House of Commons in Britain?
 A: **Standing Orders (for the conduct of proceedings till they are superseded).**

2 Q: For what sporting event is the city of 'Le Mans' famous?
 A: **Motor racing (in France; annual motor race).**

3 Q: Into which ocean does the Mackenzie river flow?
 A: **Arctic Ocean (accept Beaufort Sea, in Canada).**

4 Q: A 'descent' is the collective noun for what type of bird?
 A: **Woodpeckers.**

QUIZ 2
ROUND SIX
(Team Questions)

1 Q: What are the very thin high heels of women's shoes called?
 A: **Stilettos.**

2 Q: The English footballer, Peter Shilton, left Leicester City in 1974 to join which club?
 A: **Stoke City.**

3 Q: Which 1976 film, starring Robert Redford and Dustin Hoffman, dealt with the uncovering of the Watergate Scandal?
 A: **'All the Presidents' Men'.**

4 Q: Which English King died at the Battle of Bosworth Field?
 A: **Richard III.**

QUIZ 3
ROUND SIX
(Team Questions)

1 Q: The assassination of Archduke Ferdinand of Austria, set off a chain events which led to what?
 A: **World War I.**

2 Q: Which composer wrote the music for the ballet 'Billy the Kid' in 1938?
 A: **Aaron Copland (U.S. composer, born 1900).**

3 Q: In which film did Roger Moore make his debut as James Bond?
A: **'Live and Let Die' (in 1973).**

4 Q: Near which town in England is Anne Hathaway's cottage?
A: **Stratford upon Avon (in a village called Shottery; wife of William Shakespeare).**

QUIZ 4
ROUND SIX
(Team Questions)

1 Q: The first open tennis tournament in the world, with pro players as well as amateurs, was held in Britain in 1968. In which town?
A: **It was the British Hard Courts Championship at Bournemouth, won by Ken Rosewall of Australia.**

2 Q: How did Mrs. Davina Thompson make medical history in December 1986?
A: **She became the world's first triple-transplant patient (heart, lungs and liver).**

3 Q: What is the capital town of the Scilly Isles, on St. Mary's Isle?
A: **Hugh Town.**

4 Q: Which explorer sailed in a ship called the 'Santa Maria'?
A: **Christopher Columbus.**

QUIZ 5
ROUND SIX
(Team Questions)

1 Q: Which member of the royal family is to take part in 'Sporting Weekends with the English Gentry', as sold to American Tourists for 1987?
A: **Captain Mark Phillips.**

2 Q: Who were the French brothers who patented the cinematographe in 1895?
A: **Lumiere.**

3 Q: What was special about the shape of the bomber aircraft the Avro Vulcan?
A: **First large bomber to utilise the Delta Wing configuration (Triangular).**

4 Q: Which king was on the English throne when Bonnie Prince Charlie was defeated at the battle of Culloden?
A: **George II (1746).**

QUIZ 1
ROUND SIX
(Team Questions)

1 Q: What is the name given to the Pastoral staff or crook of a Bishop?
   A: **Crozier (a staff surmounted by a crook or cross).**

2 Q: What is the popular name of the Australian National Rugby Union team?
   A: **'The Wallabies'.**

3 Q: Into which sea does the Volga river flow?
   A: **Caspian (in the W. Soviet Union).**

4 Q: A 'plump' is the collective noun for what type of bird?
   A: **Moorhens (or ducks, wildfowl).**

QUIZ 2
ROUND SIX
(Team Questions)

1 Q: What shape was a traditional 'cocked hat'?
   A: **Triangular (with three points formed by turned up brims).**

2 Q: From which English soccer club did Brian Greenhof come before he joined Leeds United?
   A: **Manchester United.**

3 Q: Which 1969 film about the sleazy side of New York starred Dustin Hoffman and Jon Voight?
   A: **'Midnight Cowboy'.**

4 Q: Which English King was defeated at the Battle of Naseby?
   A: **Charles I (Charles Stuart in 1645; during the Civil War, defeated by the Parliamentarians).**

QUIZ 3
ROUND SIX
(Team Questions)

1 Q: What is the children's rhyme 'Ring-a Ring-o-Roses' thought to refer to?
   A: **The Black Death (or Great Plague because of the coughing and sneezing symptoms).**

2 Q: Which composer wrote the opera 'Billy Budd' in 1951?
   A: **Benjamin Britten (English composer, and pianist died 1976).**

3 Q: Whose film breakthrough came with his portrayal of a drunken young lawyer in the film 'Easy Rider'?
A: **Jack Nicholson (1969).**

4 Q: In which English county is the Glyndebourne Opera House located, at which an annual festival is held?
A: **East Sussex (founded by John Christie in 1934).**

QUIZ 4
ROUND SIX
(Team Questions)

1 Q: Which tennis player won both the American and Wimbledon mens singles finals in 1955 without dropping a single set?
A: **Tony Trabert of the United States.**

2 Q: Which anniversary was celebrated by Esperanto speakers in 1987?
A: **One hundred years since it's first publication (accept 'invention').**

3 Q: In which Swiss town was the International Red Cross Society established in 1864?
A: **Geneva.**

4 Q: Which well known person sailed in a ship called the 'Terra Nova'?
A: **Captain Scott.**

QUIZ 5
ROUND SIX
(Team Questions)

1 Q: Captain Phillips is to help manage a three million pound Scottish equestrian centre, in which famous sporting locality?
A: **Gleneagles.**

2 Q: Who were the French brothers who made the first ascent in a hot-air balloon?
A: **Montgolfier.**

3 Q: What was the name given to the large German rocket powered missile used in World War II, especially to bombard London?
A: **V2.**

4 Q: At which battle was Henry VII informally crowned in 1485?
A: **Bosworth.**

QUIZ 1
ROUND SEVEN
(Individual Questions: No conferring by either side)

1 Q: In what way is the Latin phrase 'exempli gratia' more familiar to us?
  A: By it's initials e.g. (for example).

2 Q: For what kind of painting did the English artist John Constable become most famous?
  A: Landscapes (English rural landscapes especially; 1776–1837).

3 Q: Which actor was star of the 1984 U.S. film, 'The Natural', about a baseball hero?
  A: Robert Redford.

4 Q: Who was Alexander the Great's famous tutor?
  A: Aristotle (the Greek philosopher during the 4th century).

QUIZ 2
ROUND SEVEN
(Individual Questions: No conferring by either side)

1 Q: Ulan Bator is the capital city of which country?
  A: Mongolian Peoples Republic (in E. Central Asia).

2 Q: Who was the girl famous for officiating on the British TV entertainment series the 'Golden Shot'?
  A: Anne Aston.

3 Q: For how many years does a British copyright legally last?
  A: Fifty years from death of an author or composer.

4 Q: Who was born in Norfolk, England in 1737, became connected with rights of man, ranging from slavery to U.S. Independence and died in New York in 1809?
  A: Thomas Paine. (Works include the pamphlets 'Common Sense' 1776 and 'The Rights of Man' 1791).

QUIZ 3
ROUND SEVEN
(Individual Questions: No conferring by either side)

1 Q: What was the Russian assembly (parliament) called before the Revolution of 1917?
  A: The Duma (Dooma) established by Tsar Nicholas II in 1905).

2 Q: Which racehorse trainer set a postwar Royal Ascot record with seven winners in June 1987?
   A: **Henry Cecil (the previous postwar best was six by Vincent O'Brien in 1975).**

3 Q: What is the most common tuberous-rooted food crop of this country?
   A: **The potato.**

4 Q: What is the primary concern of a member of the Howard League in Britain?
   A: **Prison Reform (after John Howard, English prison reformer of the 18th century).**

QUIZ 4
ROUND SEVEN
(Individual Questions: No conferring by either side)

1 Q: When a pestle (pest-l) and mortar are used in a laboratory, for what purpose is the pestle used?
   A: **To mix or grind substances into fine pieces in the mortar.**

2 Q: Which Briton won the World Motor Racing Championship in 1976?
   A: **James Hunt.**

3 Q: Which king founded the Royal Academy (of Arts) in London?
   A: **George III (in 1768).**

4 Q: In the opera, 'Madame Butterfly' by Puccini, the tenor Pinkerton is a lieutenant in what navy?
   A: **U.S.A.**

QUIZ 5
ROUND SEVEN
(Individual Questions: No conferring by either side)

1 Q: What is the name of the golf course near Southport Lancashire, that is on the rota for staging the Open championships?
   A: **Royal Birkdale.**

2 Q: To qualify under normal circumstances for the Government's Cold Weather Payment, to what average level does the temperature have to fall?
   A: **-1.5 degrees Celsius (over seven days).**

3 Q: By what name is the tree Salix Babylonica better known (say-licks bab-ee-lon-icker)?
   A: **Weeping Willow.**

4 Q: Who was elected as MP for the parliamentary constituency of North Devon in 1974?
   A: **Jeremy Thorpe (Liberal).**

QUIZ 1
ROUND SEVEN
(Individual Questions: No conferring by either side)

1 Q: For what purpose is the French phrase 'Poste Restante' used in Britain?
  A: **Letters so addressed are kept at the Post Office until called for.**

2 Q: Which French artist made his name with his posters advertising 'Les Follies Bergeres' in Paris?
  A: **Toulouse-Lautrec (Henri, 1864—1901).**

3 Q: Which actor was star of the 1984 U.S. film, 'Tight-rope', about a mass murderer in New Orleans?
  A: **Clint Eastwood.**

4 Q: Who was the author friend of James Boswell about whom he wrote a biography?
  A: **Dr. Samuel Johnson (18th century, both members of the Literary Club founded in 1764).**

QUIZ 2
ROUND SEVEN
(Individual Questions: No conferring by either side)

1 Q: By what name was the territory of Namibia formerly known from 1919 onwards?
  A: **South West Africa (called German South West Africa before 1919).**

2 Q: What does Arthur Daley call his wife in the British TV series 'Minder'?
  A: **'Er Indoors.**

3 Q: What is meant by the literary phrase 'To Bowdlerise'?
  A: **To edit out indecent passages or words, to censor, or expurgate (after Thomas Bowdler of 18th cent.).**

4 Q: Which French philosopher, playwright and novelist who died in 1980 was the leading French exponent of aesthetic existentialism?
  A: **Jean Paul Sartre (works include 'Being and Nothingness' 1943 and the novel 'Nausea' 1938).**

QUIZ 3
ROUND SEVEN
(Individual Questions: No conferring by either side)

1 Q: What was the 'Balfour Declaration' of 1917?
  A: **A statement made by the U.K. Foreign Sec. (J. Balfour) supporting the Jewish case for a home in Palestine.**

2 Q: Which jockey rode a record eight winners at Royal Ascot in 1965 and again in 1975?
  A: **Lester Piggott.**

3 Q: Laver and Dulse are edible types of which plant?
  A: **Seaweed.**

4 Q: 'Carthusians' are the old boys from which public school in England?
  A: **Charterhouse School (Godalming, Surrey).**

QUIZ 4
ROUND SEVEN
(Individual Questions: No conferring by either side)

1 Q: What is a better known name for phenol (fee-nol), a powerful antiseptic and strong disinfectant?
  A: **Carbolic Acid.**

2 Q: What was the nationality of 1979 World Racing Champion Jody Scheckter?
  A: **South African.**

3 Q: Who designed the Royal Hospital, Chelsea, London?
  A: **Christopher Wren (completed in 1685; founded by Charles II in 1682).**

4 Q: What type of role was the English stage actress Sarah Siddons famous for portraying?
  A: **Tragedy.**

QUIZ 5
ROUND SEVEN
(Individual Questions: No conferring by either side)

1 Q: What is the name of the golf course near Blackpool Lancashire, that is on the rota for staging the Open championships?
  A: **Royal Lytham & St. Annes.**

2 Q: The seven day period of qualification for the Government's Cold Weather Payment, has to start on which day of the week?
  A: **Monday.**

3 Q: What are seeds of the Aesculus Hippocastanum tree commonly known as (ees-cue-lus hippo-cass-tarnum)?
   A: **Conkers (or horse chestnuts).**

4 Q: Who was elected as MP for the parliamentary constituency Huyton in Lancashire, in 1974?
   A: **Harold Wilson (Labour).**

QUIZ 1
ROUND EIGHT
(Team Questions)

1 Q: Writer, Edgar Allan Poe, frequently wrote with what balanced on his left shoulder?
A: **His pet cat.**

2 Q: In which century was the game of bowls, played on grass, started in Britain?
A: **13th century.**

3 Q: The man-eating bellowing monster inhabiting swamps and lagoons called the 'Bunyip' is featured in the folk-lore of which country?
A: **Australia (aboriginal).**

4 Q: Which English monarch was buried in a square coffin?
A: **Queen Anne (1665–1714).**

QUIZ 2
ROUND EIGHT
(Team Questions)

1 Q: Burlington House, in London has been the home of what since 1868?
A: **Royal Academy of Arts.**

2 Q: Which member of the clergy would live in a 'Manse'?
A: **A Presbyterian Minister.**

3 Q: Which famous actor was narrator for the 1963 film 'Zulu' set during Rorke's Drift battle in 1879?
A: **Richard Burton.**

4 Q: Name an English county which is famous for it's Fens, other than Norfolk?
A: **Lincolnshire or Cambridgeshire (reclaimed flat marshland of East England).**

QUIZ 3
ROUND EIGHT
(Team Questions)

1 Q: From what is 'semolina', used in milk pudding desserts made?
A: **Wheat, after flour has been bolted.**

2 Q: What was the name of the Roman god of sleep which is perpetuated in an English word meaning sleepy or drowsy?
A: **Somnus (Somnolent).**

3 Q: What regulating body is represented by the letters
   B.B.B.C. in Britain?
 A: **British Boxing Board of Control.**

4 Q: What famous London landmark is topped by a
   seventeen feet high statue sculptured by E.H. Baily?
 A: **Nelson's Column (Trafalgar Square).**

QUIZ 4
ROUND EIGHT
(Team Questions)

1 Q: What city is co-extensive with the District of
   Colombia in the U.S.A.?
 A: **Washington (D.C.; capital of the U.S.)**

2 Q: What is meant by a person's 'alter ego'?
 A: **Other self, another self or a very close friend or
   intimate friend (from the Latin).**

3 Q: Which actor starred in the 1971 film 'Get Carter'?
 A: **Michael Caine.**

4 Q: Name the large bottle in which Champagne is sold
   that is equal to twenty bottles?
 A: **Nebuchadnezzer (named after the Old Testament
   King of Babylon).**

QUIZ 5
ROUND EIGHT
(Team Questions)

1 Q: What, in the Moslem world, are Minarets?
 A: **Tall, slender towers on a Mosque.**

2 Q: Which country was admitted to the Commonwealth
   in 1972, and the United Nations two years later?
 A: **Bangladesh (formerly part of Pakistan).**

3 Q: Which medical word describes a deficiency of
   Haemoglobin, the Oxygen-carrying pigment in red
   cells?
 A: **Anaemia.**

4 Q: Who was the male star of the 1978 film 'Grease',
   about true love in the fifties?
 A: **John Travolta.**

QUIZ 1
ROUND EIGHT
(Team Questions)

1 Q: What item of clothing or accessory did the wife of Napoleon III, the Empress Eugenie, never wear more than twice?
  A: **Shoes.**

2 Q: Which is traditionally the most popular card game in Britain?
  A: **Bridge.**

3 Q: According to legend which is said to be the only animal immune from the deathly gaze of the cockatrice or basilisk monster?
  A: **Weasel (which could also kill it).**

4 Q: Which famous 19th century woman carried a pet owl in her pocket everywhere she went?
  A: **Florence Nightingale.**

QUIZ 2
ROUND EIGHT
(Team Questions)

1 Q: In which part of London is the National Portrait Gallery located?
  A: **North side of Trafalgar Square, in St. Martin's Place (adjoining National Gallery).**

2 Q: A 'mercator projection' is most likely to be found on what?
  A: **On a map or atlas (after Mercator, a Flemish cartographer of the 16th century).**

3 Q: Which famous actor was narrator for the 1962 epic film 'How the West was Won'?
  A: **Spencer Tracy.**

4 Q: Ennerdale Water, Crummock and Hawes are part of which area in England?
  A: **The Lake District, Cumbria (lakes in the region).**

QUIZ 3
ROUND EIGHT
(Team Questions)

1 Q: What is sago, as used in milk pudding desserts?
  A: **Starchy cereal obtained from the pith of the sago palm tree (found in tropical Asia).**

Q: In which country of the world would you find adherents of the ancient 'Coptic Church'?
A: **Egypt or Ethiopia.**

3 Q: What regulating body is represented by the letters B.B.F.C. in Britain?
A: **British Board of Film Censors.**

4 Q: Who re-built the Brighton Pavilion from 1815–1823?
A: **John Nash (English town planner).**

QUIZ 4
ROUND EIGHT
(Team Questions)

1 Q: What is the capital of the state of Hawaii, in the U.S.A.?
A: **Honolulu (part of S. Oahu Island).**

2 Q: What is meant by a 'sequestered' life?
A: **Retired into seclusion, isolated.**

3 Q: Which actor starred in the 1958 comedy film 'Lucky Jim'?
A: **Ian Carmichael (as an accident prone junior lecturer of a University).**

4 Q: What value has the number described as a googol in mathematics?
A: **The number ten to power of hundred (i.e. one followed by one hundred zeroes; 10–100).**

QUIZ 5
ROUND EIGHT
(Team Questions)

1 Q: What function is performed in the Muslim world, by the Mufti?
A: **They are experts in legal matters.**

2 Q: Which country became a member of the Commonwealth in 1948, and a Republic in 1972?
A: **Sri Lanka (it's name means 'Resplendent Island').**

3 Q: What name is given to the inherited disease in which one of the factors needed for blood clotting is missing?
A: **Haemophilia.**

4 Q: Which famous singer made his screen debut, in 1959 in the film 'Serious Charge'?
A: **Cliff Richard.**

QUIZ 1
FRIENDLY QUESTIONS

1 Q: The leaf-shoots of which plant are called English Bamboo, after being boiled as a substitute for Asparagus?
  A: **Elder (other old recipes include Elder flower vinegar, fritters, gruel and skin ointments).**

2 Q: 'Sea-parrot' is an old sailor's name for what creature?
  A: **Puffin.**

3 Q: British soldiers who had been training in which African country were the centre of an AIDS scare in January 1987?
  A: **Kenya.**

4 Q: What is the special property of a catalyst in chemical reactions?
  A: **While having an increasing rate of chemical reaction it is not usually changed permanently itself.**

MORE FRIENDLY QUESTIONS

1 Q: What is a 'sinecure' (sin-e-cur)?
  A: **It is an office or position with salary but with few or no duties to perform.**

2 Q: What is the other name for the musical instrument the 'mouth-organ'?
  A: **Harmonica (small wind instrument with reeds).**

3 Q: What line follows 'Tho cowards flinch and traitors sneer' from a well known song?
  A: **'We'll keep the Red Flag flying here' (the Red Flag socialist song written by James Connell 1889).**

4 Q: In the Bible, on what day did God create the Sun, Moon and stars?
  A: **Fourth day.**

RESERVE QUESTIONS

1 Q: The actresses Sharon Gless and Tyne Daley star as police in which American T.V. series?
  A: **'Cagney and Lacey'.**

2 Q: Which nation administers the territory of the Commonwealth of Puerto Rico?
  A: **U.S.A. (in the Greater Antilles, Caribbean - ceded by Spain in 1899).**

QUIZ 1
FRIENDLY QUESTIONS

1 Q: Which bird's nests are used to make bird's-nest soup?
   A: **Swift or Swallow.**

2 Q: What creature was referred to by sailors as a 'sea-dog'?
   A: **Seal.**

3 Q: Which London Borough was revealed in January 1987 as having the highest rate of illegitimate births in the country?
   A: **Lambeth (430 in every 1,000).**

4 Q: What dangerous gas is given off in a blast furnace during manufacture of pig-iron?
   A: **Carbon Monoxide.**

MORE FRIENDLY QUESTIONS

1 Q: What are 'Dundrearies'?
   A: **Long side whiskers worn without beard.**

2 Q: What does a first-nighter do?
   A: **Attends the first nights of plays (opening performances).**

3 Q: Which politician said, 'When you stop a dictator there are always risks. But there are greater risks in not stopping a dictator'?
   A: **Margaret Thatcher.**

4 Q: Who, in the Bible, was asked to interpret the 'Writing on the Wall'?
   A: **Daniel (at King Belshazzar's request).**

RESERVE QUESTIONS

1 Q: The actors Karl Malden and Michael Douglas starred together as police in which American T.V. series?
   A: **'The Streets of San Francisco'.**

2 Q: What is the name of the Black Sea's only outlet?
   A: **The Bosphorus (between European and Asian Turkey).**

QUIZ 2
FRIENDLY QUESTIONS

1 Q: Which football league team play their home games at Roker Park?
  A: **Sunderland.**

2 Q: What did Mr. Elie Wiesel (vee-ssel) receive at a ceremony at Oslo University in December 1986?
  A: **The Nobel Peace Prize.**

3 Q: In computer terminology, the smallest unit of information is called a bit. How is the word 'bit' derived?
  A: **Short for 'Binary Digit'.**

4 Q: What is the stretch of water between Sweden and Denmark called?
  A: **The Kattegat.**

MORE FRIENDLY QUESTIONS

1 Q: The German philosopher Gottfried Leibniz and Isaac Newton independently developed which 17th century innovation in mathematics?
  A: **Calculus (differential. Leibniz was accused of plagiarism, but his ideas were original).**

2 Q: What was the profession of the acknowledged master, Auguste Escoffier?
  A: **Chef (at the Grand, Monte Carlo, The Savoy, London and the Carlton; creator of Peach Melba in 1893).**

3 Q: What sort of things have the following as notable examples, The Great Mogul, The Orlov, and The Jonker?
  A: **Diamonds.**

4 Q: Mr. William Casey collapsed in December 1986 when about to give the U.S. Congress further information about 'Irangate'. What position did he hold?
  A: **Director of the C.I.A.**

RESERVE QUESTIONS

1 Q: What sport has the Latin name of 'Toxophily'?
  A: **Archery (the Royal Toxophilite Society was founded in 1981).**

2 Q: Who lead the Peasant's Revolt in 1381?
  A: **Wat Tyler (the first major revolt of the lower classes in English history).**

QUIZ 2
FRIENDLY QUESTIONS

1 Q: Which second division team beat Manchester United to win the F.A. Cup in 1976?
  A: **Southampton.**

2 Q: The writer of one of the best known poems of World War II, 'The Naming of Parts', and of many radio plays, died in December 1986. Who was he?
  A: **Henry Reed.**

3 Q: Many computers process eight bits as a single unit known as a byte. What is the computer term for half a byte, or four bits?
  A: **A Nibble.**

4 Q: What is the stretch of water between Norway and Denmark called?
  A: **Skaggerak.**

MORE FRIENDLY QUESTIONS

1 Q: Who independently proposed the principle of natural selection at the same time as Charles Darwin?
  A: **Alfred Russell Wallace (the idea was jointly presented in a paper to the Linnean Society, 1858).**

2 Q: What was the profession of the Frenchman, Emmanuel Poire, who, under the pseudonym Caran D'Ache, became one of the earliest exponents of his art?
  A: **Cartoonist, illustrator and caricaturist.**

3 Q: Which diamond, discovered in 1905, was cut to provide the two 'Stars of Africa' of the crown jewels?
  A: **Cullinan (the stars, one on the sceptre, one on the crown, are the largest cut stones in the world.**

4 Q: Dr. Davis Wilson was appointed by the Queen in January 1987 to be probably the last Governor of where?
  A: **Hong Kong.**

RESERVE QUESTIONS

1 Q: The name of which sport, literally translated, means 'Empty Hand'?
  A: **Karate.**

2 Q: Who led the Fenland Rebellion against William I in 1070?
  A: **Hereward the Wake.**

QUIZ 3
FRIENDLY QUESTIONS

1 Q: How many sisters complete the name of the well known North London Road?
   A: **Seven (Seven Sisters Road).**

2 Q: In which 1978 BBC TV series did the characters Anna Newcross, Sarah Lloyd-Smith and Jay Harper feature?
   A: **'Angels' (hospital soap opera).**

3 Q: If your 24 hour clock was 35 minutes slow and showed the time as 1750 hours, how long would you have, to keep an appointment at 6.30 p.m.?
   A: **Five minutes.**

4 Q: Which fictional bear was the hero of a book by Richard Adams?
   A: **Shardik (1974).**

MORE FRIENDLY QUESTIONS

1 Q: If you were in a French restaurant and ordered 'pommes de terre frites' what would you get?
   A: **Chips.**

2 Q: Apart from being names, 'Gilbert', 'Marshall', 'Solomon', 'Caroline' and 'Mariana', are all types of what?
   A: **Islands (groups of).**

3 Q: Which American film actor has starred in the films 'M.A.S.H.' (1970), 'Klute' (1971), and 'Don't Look Now' (1973)?
   A: **Donald Sutherland.**

4 Q: What type of musical instrument is a 'Marimba'?
   A: **Primative xylophone used in Latin America, originating in West Africa.**

RESERVE QUESTIONS

1 Q: In which Polish city is the second oldest university in Central Europe, where the astronomer Copernicus was a student?
   A: **Krakow (university 1364).**

2 Q: Who recorded the song 'Little Arrows' in 1968?
   A: **Leapy Lee (reached No.2 in U.K. charts).**

QUIZ 3
FRIENDLY QUESTIONS

1 Q: Give the colloquial name of London's Middlesex Street, site of a popular market?
  A: **Petticoat Lane.**

2 Q: Who is the actress who originally played the mother 'that makes three' in the BBC TV comedy series of the 70s?
  A: **Wendy Craig ('Mother Makes Three').**

3 Q: If you paid two hundred and thirty pounds for an item that included 15% V.A.T. how much would the same thing have cost without V.A.T.?
  A: **Two hundred pounds.**

4 Q: Which author wrote the novel 'De la terre a la lune' (in which he stated that Cape Kennedy would be used for shooting a capsule to the moon)?
  A: **Jules Verne (French novelist 1828–1905).**

MORE FRIENDLY QUESTIONS

1 Q: What kind of food is the French dish vichyssoise (vee-see-swah)?
  A: **Thick soup of potato and leek usually served chilled.**

2 Q: One word signifies the following; a military weapon, a type of cement, an article used by a chemist. What is the word?
  A: **Mortar.**

3 Q: Which American film actor has starred in the films 'Kotch' (1971), 'Charley Varrick' (1973), and 'The Sunshine Boys' (1975)?
  A: **Walter Matthau.**

4 Q: On which musical instrument would you be most likely to play a 'pibroch' (pea-brock)?
  A: **Scottish Bagpipes (theme and variations specially for the bagpipes).**

RESERVE QUESTIONS

1 Q: What is the name of the game reserve in North East Transvaal, South Africa, situated between the Limpopo river and Komatipoort?
  A: **Kruger National Park.**

2 Q: Who recorded the song 'Little Children' in 1964?
  A: **Billy J. Kramer and the Dakotas (reached No. 1).**

QUIZ 4
FRIENDLY QUESTIONS

1 Q: What is a person described as an apostate?
   A: **One who renounces religious vows, abandons
       their religion, party or cause etc.**

2 Q: What does a gallon of water weigh, in pounds?
   A: **Ten pounds.**

3 Q: Which island are the Grand Banks Fishing grounds
       nearest to?
   A: **Newfoundland (off E. Canada).**

4 Q: Complete the following well known proverb: 'Don't
       hide your light. . . . .'?
   A: **'. . . . . Under a Bushel' (meaning don't conceal
       your talents).**

MORE FRIENDLY QUESTIONS

1 Q: What is a 'whetstone' used for primarily?
   A: **Sharpening tools (especially edged tools or
       knives).**

2 Q: In which American state would you find the town of
       San Diego?
   A: **California (port on the Pacific).**

3 Q: Who was the author of the romantic novel, 'The
       Master of Ballantrae'?
   A: **Robert Louis Stevenson (Scottish author, written
       1889).**

4 Q: In which Mozart opera does the High Priest Sarasto
       address the aria 'O Isis and Osiris' to the Ancient
       Egyptian Gods?
   A: **'The Magic Flute'.**

RESERVE QUESTIONS

1 Q: What is the name of the international daily
       newspaper of the religious group, The Christian
       Scientists?
   A: **''Christian Science Monitor'.**

2 Q: What is the original name given to the art of applying
       cut out designs and patterned materials to any
       surface to create an attractive pattern?
   A: **Decoupage (dee-coup-aj — collage is the twentieth
       century offshoot of this).**

QUIZ 4
FRIENDLY QUESTIONS

1 Q: What is a person described as a proselyte (prossy-lite)?
A: **One who is converted to religious faith, especially a gentile to Judaism.**

2 Q: What is the equivalent temperature in degrees Fahrenheit of 100 degrees centigrade?
A: **212 degrees F (the temperature at which water boils).**

3 Q: In which country is the city of Sao Paulo?
A: **Brazil (largest city and industrial centre in Brazil).**

4 Q: Complete the following well known proverb: 'To kill the goose that laid. . . . . . .'?
A: **'. . . . . . .the Golden Eggs' (meaning to sacrifice future rewards for present gains).**

MORE FRIENDLY QUESTIONS

1 Q: What was the name given to the coal wagons immediately attached to steam railway engines?
A: **Tender.**

2 Q: Who planned the American city of Philadelphia in the 1680s?
A: **William Penn (English quaker — founder of the original colony there).**

3 Q: Name the novel written by Alan Sillitoe, in 1959 about a boy in a Borstal.
A: **'The Loneliness of the Long Distance Runner'.**

4 Q: Which was Wagner's last opera in 1881 that includes the 'Good Friday Music'?
A: **'Parsifal'.**

RESERVE QUESTIONS

1 Q: What is the official publication of the religious group the Jehovah's Witnesses?
A: **Watch Tower.**

2 Q: What is the name given to the art of decorating or engraving the bones and ivory of whales and walruses?
A: **Scrimshaw (originally done by sailors as a leisure activity).**

QUIZ 5
FRIENDLY QUESTIONS

1 Q: What was discovered at Rum Jungle, Northern
   Australia in 1952?
   A: Uranium.

2 Q: The Englishman Peter Collins was World Champion
   in 1976, in what sport?
   A: Speedway.

3 Q: What is a hunt which follows an artificial trail or scent
   instead of a live animal called?
   A: A Drag Hunt.

4 Q: What was rationalised as a result of the Jenkins
   report of 1962?
   A: The Stock Exchange (reduced the 21 provincial
   exchanges to the five regional ones).

MORE FRIENDLY QUESTIONS

1 Q: In the international C.G.S. measurement system,
   what does the initial 'S' represent?
   A: Second (centimetre — gramme).

2 Q: Who was the American baseball star at one time
   married to Marilyn Monroe?
   A: Joe Di Maggio.

3 Q: Which nation built the ocean liner 'Normandie' in
   1931?
   A: France.

4 Q: What is the opposite of Centrifugal, as in centrifugal
   force?
   A: Centripetal (moving towards a centre).

RESERVE QUESTIONS

1 Q: Who originally played the part of Brother Dominic in
   the British TV series 'Oh Brother' in 1970?
   A: Derek Nimmo.

2 Q: Of what American state is Baton Rouge the capital?
   A: Louisiana (Southern U.S. on the Gulf of Mexico).

QUIZ 5
FRIENDLY QUESTIONS

1 Q: What is the highest waterfall in the world?
   A: **Angel Falls (Venezuala 3,211 feet).**

2 Q: The 'Cincinati Reds' team were World Champions
       in 1975 and 76, in what sport?
   A: **Baseball.**

3 Q: What are 'snaffles' and 'pelhams'?
   A: **Types of horse bits.**

4 Q: What is the French equivalent of the Stock Exchange
       called?
   A: **The Bourse.**

MORE FRIENDLY QUESTIONS

1 Q: In physics, what is the heat required to raise one
       gramme of water one degree centigrade called?
   A: **A calorie.**

2 Q: Who is the American film star married to the tennis
       player John McEnroe?
   A: **Tatum O'Neal.**

3 Q: Which nation re-built the famous transatlantic ocean
       liner the 'Bremen' in 1955?
   A: **Germany (originally owned by France and named
       the 'Pasteur').**

4 Q: What is the opposite of fission, as in nuclear fission?
   A: **Fusion (combining or melting together).**

RESERVE QUESTIONS

1 Q: Name the animated dog who starred in the children's
       TV programme 'Magic Roundabout' in the 1960s.
   A: **Dougal (created by Serge Danot).**

2 Q: Of what American state is Charleston the capital?
   A: **West Virginia (eastern U.S.; formerly part of
       Virginia before Civil War).**

A SELECTED LIST OF REFERENCE TITLES AVAILABLE FROM CORGI BOOKS

THE PRICES SHOWN BELOW WERE CORRECT AT THE TIME OF GOING TO PRESS. HOWEVER TRANSWORLD PUBLISHERS RESERVE THE RIGHT TO SHOW NEW RETAIL PRICES ON COVERS WHICH MAY DIFFER FROM THOSE PREVIOUSLY ADVERTISED IN THE TEXT OR ELSEWHERE.

☐ 07200 1	Test Yourself (I.Q.)	*William Bernard & Jules Leopold*	£1.95
☐ 99234 8	En Route: French Autoroute Guide	*Richard Binns*	£3.95
☐ 99230 5	Hidden France	*Richard Binns*	£3.95
☐ 99231 3	France A La Carte	*Richard Binns*	£3.95
☐ 99232 1	French Leave	*Richard Binns*	£4.95
☐ 99233 X	Richard Binns' Best of Britain	*Richard Binns*	£3.95
☐ 13339 6	The Pub Quiz Book	*Burns & Porter*	£1.95
☐ 13398 1	The Pub Quiz Book 2	*Burns & Porter*	£1.99
☐ 13399 X	The Pub Quiz Book 3	*Burns & Porter*	£1.99
☐ 11001 9	Great War Speeches		
		Sir Winston Churchill, K.G., O.M., C.H., M.P.	£2.50
☐ 12733 7	Family Favourites: Your Holiday Guide		
		R. Dewhurst & G. Thomas	£4.95
☐ 12772 8	Know Your Own PSI-Q	*Hans Eysenck & Carl Sargent*	£2.50
☐ 12479 6	Doctors	*Jonathan Gathorne-Hardy*	£4.95
☐ 12555 5	In Search of Schrodinger's Cat	*John Gribbin*	£3.95
☐ 12656 X	In Search of the Double Helix	*John Gribbin*	£4.95
☐ 13053 2	Linkword Language Course In French	*Dr. M. Gruneberg*	£3.95
☐ 13054 0	Linkword Language Course In German	*Dr. M. Gruneberg*	£3.95
☐ 13055 9	Linkword Language Course In Spanish	*Dr. M. Gruneberg*	£3.95
☐ 13056 7	Linkword Language Course In Italian	*Dr. M. Gruneberg*	£3.95
☐ 13409 0	New Corgi Crossword Puzzle Book 1	*Russell & Carter*	£1.95
☐ 13410 4	New Corgi Crossword Puzzle Book 2	*Russell & Carter*	£1.95
☐ 13332 9	Trivial Pursuit: The Authorized Game Book		£6.95

All Corgi/Bantam Books are available at your bookshop or newsagent, or can be ordered from the following address:
Corgi/Bantam Books,
Cash Sales Department,
P.O. Box 11, Falmouth, Cornwall TR10 9EN

Please send a cheque or postal order (no currency) and allow 60p for postage and packing for the first book plus 25p for the second book and 15p for each additional book ordered up to a maximum charge of £1.90 in UK.

B.F.P.O. customers please allow 60p for the first book, 25p for the second book plus 15p per copy for the next 7 books, thereafter 9p per book.

Overseas customers, including Eire, please allow £1.25 for postage and packing for the first book, 75p for the second book, and 28p for each subsequent title ordered.

NAME (Block Letters) ....

ADDRESS ....

....